Assembly Stories from Around the World

Assemblies for Secondary Schools

Richard and Philip Hughes

Oxford University Press 1989

Oxford University Press, Walton Street, Oxford OX2 6DP

Oxford New York Toronto
Melbourne Auckland
Petaling Jaya Singapore Hong Kong Tokyo
Delhi Bombay Calcutta Madras Karachi
Nairobi Dar es Salaam Cape Town

and associated companies in
Berlin Ibadan

Oxford is a trade mark of Oxford University Press
© Richard Hughes 1989
First published 1989

ISBN 0 19 917104 1

Printed and bound in Great Britain by
Butler & Tanner Ltd, Frome and London

Contents

Introduction

Particular communions teach their own highly developed religious traditions. The experience of being brought up as a member of an orthodox Jewish family, for instance, or as a loyal member of the Roman Catholic Church, can affect a person's outlook for life. But a school is not a church, a synagogue or a mosque. And many schools have little more than tenuous connexions with such real communities of faith and worship. The majority of schools and their teachers are not therefore bound to any particular set of religious values, nor is there a similar emotional and spiritual commitment within a school as can be found in the households of faith. So what is to be said at school assemblies? And what meaning is there, if any, to an act of communal worship in the school? It is not easy to supply coherent answers to such questions.

Yet it is a sign of the times that even schools with a specific religious affiliation are nowadays anxious to inculcate a spirit of racial and religious tolerance. It has led, in recent years, to a greater and greater emphasis on a multi-faith approach to religious education. In this, schools can play a distinctive role. Knowledge, understanding and tolerance of the different religious persuasions can be promoted by the school. In some places, where there is a mix of pupils of different backgrounds, it has the added advantage of benefiting the school community. And it is seen generally as a significant contribution to racial and religious harmony within our present pluralistic society.

Many assembly and classroom books have been devoted to this development. But there is, I believe, an alternative approach, and that germane to education itself. The history of ideas is the staple diet of education, and supplies a fertile breeding ground from which new observations can be made. Yet education is in serious danger of neglecting the contribution made by religion to our intellectual traditions. It may be argued that we live in a post-Christian era, but we remain nevertheless within traditions of thought in which religion has played a very significant part. No study of Renaissance Drama, Pre-Raphaelite Art, Mediaeval History — indeed of seventeenth century Chemistry or Mathematics — can entirely be intelligible without a knowledge of such religious ideas. To be ignorant of them is, I believe, to be less than educated. Yet there is an undoubted tendency in our schools to neglect such knowledge, thus dispossessing our pupils of a significant part of their cultural heritage.

This book has been prepared with that heritage in mind. It consists of groups of school assemblies, organized chronologically and divided into topics. They describe contexts and ideas which, in some sense, have added to our perceptions. The first group of assemblies entitled 'The Land of Canaan', for example, supplies factual information about early developments in civilization and primitive religion. A great variety of more sophisticated modes of religious thought are illustrated in the later groups. They range from the speculations of the Greek philosophers to the examination of the relationship between faith and science in the wake of the Renaissance.

These assemblies, though, are not simply about religion. They also describe the contribution made to our knowledge by the archaeologists — Kathleen Kenyon's astonishing discoveries at Jericho for instance. They are concerned with anthropology, with art, with the development and the transmission of literature. Often, it has been possible in the course of this book, to discuss important matters not part elsewhere of the ordinary curriculum of the school. Few schools, for instance, still teach Greek or Latin. Yet our thinking owes great debts to the classics — at one time, indeed, the subjects taught in class.

Most of these assemblies do not require equipment and can be conducted by the teacher alone. There are, however, a number of them in which extra preparation is required. These are flagged * in the 'List of contents'. In most schools these days it is not practicable to bring all the pupils together each morning. It is much more usual for a particular year group to hold a communal assembly on a certain day of the week. Tutorials in class are held on other days. These are valuable exercises in helping pupils to form opinions. In the hope that these assemblies will be useful for such tutorial sessions, I have included possible questions for debate with each passage.

Richard Hughes
Whitchurch on Thames

The Land of Canaan

The Carmel Caves   (5 mins)

The flat coastal plain of the Holy Land narrows in the north, where the Carmel
Range runs across towards the sea at Haifa. The mountains form a promontory
on the coast called, since the earliest times, the Antelope's Nose. A little inland
in the base of the mountain range is a narrow cleft called the Valley of the Caves.
The Carmel Caves hang at various heights on the southern side of this valley.
It is a scramble through the prickly pears up a rough, steep track for about eighty
feet to reach the highest of them. It is called the Cave of the Oven.

Those caves were formed by water cutting into the soft, porous limestone. But
the water had ceased and people were already living in the caves thirty-thousand
years ago. Walk into the Cave of the Oven. It consists of a large central chamber
and a funnel, formed by the water, rises through the rock above. That funnel was
used by those cave dwellers as a natural chimney. You can imagine a small group
of primitive men, women and children, dressed in skins, huddled around a large
fire beneath the funnel. That fire kept them warm at night, and they used it for
cooking.

When the scholars began their study of the Cave of the Oven, they dug into
the earth of the floor of the chamber. This was the debris left by the hundreds
of generations of people who inhabited this cave. Much of the ash came from the
fires they made, and in the debris were the bones of some of the animals they
cooked − hippopotamus, gazelle, horse, ox, fallow deer. As the scholars dug deeper
and deeper, they found objects from further and further back in time. The deepest
levels were left by the earliest people of the cave. The chamber turned out to have
a depth of about fifty feet of debris!

We know so little about the people who lived in the caves. What kind of a language
did they develop? How long did it take? What customs did they have? We will
probably never know the answers. Yet the excavations made by the scholars do
give us tantalizing glimpses of their way of life. The levels at which particular
animal bones have been found tell us, for instance, what types of meat they ate

at different times and show that, over the many thousands of years during which the caves were occupied, several changes in climate occurred. Many flint implements were found. They were used for all kinds of different purposes. A flint scraper, for instance, could be used to shape an arrow. A thinner, pointed sliver of flint could then be used for the arrow head. The people who lived in these caves survived by hunting. They had not yet learnt how to grow crops.

Studies of the other caves in the Valley of the Caves have supplied the scholars with more information about these primitive people. The terrace in front of the Cave of the Oven is particularly interesting. It was used in the last period of human habitation, and the remains of very early buildings have been found. At about the same period, new types of implement began to be used — particularly sickles shaped out of flint. People were beginning to plant and to harvest crops. The sickles that have been found are fitted with bone hafts and on many of them animal heads are carved. This is the earliest form of art discovered in the caves, but the standard of workmanship is of excellent quality. The caves have supplied fascinating insights into the very early development of human life and society. They offer glimpses of the ideas and the art of those primitive cave-dwellers. Such people could not expect to live very long lives. No skeleton of a man or a woman over the age of forty has been found. There were human burials in many of the caves and also burials on the terraces.

Two different types of burial were discovered from different times. The earliest were group burials, the skeletons in a tightly flexed position, the skulls decorated with necklaces of bone. At a later period burials were done singly, the bodies only slightly flexed and the skulls without decoration. We have no real idea of the beliefs of those people of long ago. We can only guess. Yet the different methods of burial suggest that the way in which a corpse was put into the earth was an important part of their religion. As their religion developed, so did their method of burial. Probably they believed in some form of life after death. What else can we guess about their religion? The chances are that they expected their gods to help them to be successful hunters.

QUESTIONS FOR DEBATE

1. Do you think that belief in gods is natural to all human beings — or did primitive people believe in gods because there were so many things they did not understand?
2. Can you suggest reasons why the people in the caves lived for no more than forty years?

Ancient Jericho   (8 mins)

Jericho can be found about fifteen miles north of the Dead Sea, close to the steep cliffs on the west side of the valley of the Jordan. It lies over a thousand feet below sea level, the lowest city on the face of the earth. The roadsign outside modern Jericho reminds us that it is also 'The most ancient city in the world'. Most of the year there is little rainfall in the valley, but water gushes from two plentiful springs. While Jericho is surrounded by desert, the city itself stands in a rich oasis. Grapefruit, oranges and lemons grow on the trees and colourful sub-tropical flowers abound. From the earliest times the ancient city, on one of the few crossing places of the Jordan in the south, was liable to attack by wandering tribes coming into the Holy Land.

The remains of the ancient city itself take the form of a large mound. It is called Tel-es-Sultan, and rises about seventy feet above the surrounding countryside. Most of the ancient cities in the Holy Land were built on mounds because the higher ground was easier to defend. But at Jericho the entire accumulation of debris has been produced by human habitation. Most of the ancient buildings were constructed of mud-brick and, when old walls were demolished and replaced, the mound rose gradually in height. The earliest building found at Jericho is a small sanctuary from about 9,500 B.C. Probably the first people to spend time there were nomadic hunters who lived in tents but who returned time and again to their shrine.

The archaeologists have found the remains of domed circular houses at Jericho. They were built of mud-brick about one thousand, five hundred years after the hunters had established their shrine. These give evidence of the first urban life at the site. The houses were single-roomed with the interior floors dug below ground level. Flint and bone implements were found from this period. Since pottery had not yet been invented, the people used dishes and cups made of limestone. About five hundred years later, sometime around 7,500 B.C., great improvements were made. A city wall of rough stones and a massive stone tower were built. These buildings have surprised the experts. People were skilled at city planning and military organization much earlier than expected. Jericho was now densely populated with about 2,000 inhabitants. The city could not have existed without considerable skill in agriculture, and it seems likely that irrigation schemes to extend the oasis were in use.

Jericho changed hands, perhaps violently, sometime towards 7,000 B.C. The newcomers built large rectangular houses, grouped around courtyards. The walls were of mud-brick covered with a hard lime mortar. The cooking was done in the courtyards, and good quality limestone bowls and dishes were in use. The remains of two shrines have been found from this period. In one, there was a small niche which contained a carefully worked stone pillar. But ten human skulls were the most remarkable find. The features of the dead had been skilfully restored in plaster and painted in natural colours. The eyes of the dead were replaced with shells. These skulls suggest some form of ancestor worship. This civilization on the mound lasted about two thousand years, then came to an abrupt end – almost certainly as a result of an invasion.

In the centuries that followed, many newcomers arrived. Usually Jericho had been destroyed by an enemy and deserted. Then wandering tribes found the remains of the city and used the site. The development of civilization was very uneven. Newcomers, even centuries later, lacked the skills of earlier city dwellers. Some of them lived in large pits dug into the mound. Others simply put up tents. In about 3,000 B.C., a great fortified city was built. But this city too was destroyed with fire, and the next inhabitants lived in tents.

A great fortified Canaanite city was built on the mound towards the end of the nineteenth century B.C. Houses were built on terraces rising on the sides of the mound and the city was surrounded by a substantial mud-brick wall. The scholars know more about Jericho at this time than at any other period. The remains of streets and houses from the commercial quarter of the city have been discovered. Living rooms were at first floor level, with one-roomed shops below open to the street. A store of grain was found in the remains of one of the shops. At this time, a new method of fortifying cities was adopted in the Holy Land. The military engineers deliberately made the sides of the mound steeper. A layer of hard plaster was then put on the sides of the mound. It was very difficult for an enemy to climb to the city walls.

The remains of the burials from this period have survived remarkably well. A long narrow table, laden with food was placed in a tomb. The table had two legs at one end, and one leg at the other. In some tombs, beds were installed while in others the dead were laid on rush mats. Alabaster vessels, bone-decorated boxes, platters, cups and bottles were also found. The dead were buried fully clothed, with bone-decorated wooden combs in their hair. Some of them were wearing scarabs as rings or pendants. These tombs at Jericho have greatly extended our knowledge of the civilization of Canaan before biblical times.

Jericho was destroyed with fire and great violence in about 1,560 B.C. The city was then abandoned for over a century. The final Canaanite settlement on the mound lasted only a few years and the remains of it are scanty indeed. While it is dry most of the year in the Jordan valley, there is often torrential rain in the winter months. Over the centuries, the remains of the last Canaanite civilization at Jericho have gradually been washed away. The Bible tells us that the walls of this city fell down when the Israelites came in from the desert. But because of the erosion, the biblical story cannot be proved or disproved by archaeology. The main excavations on the mound at Jericho were carried out by Kathleen Kenyon, a famous British archaeologist.

QUESTIONS FOR DEBATE

1. What do you think were the most fascinating discoveries at the site of the most ancient city on earth?
2. Why do you think people went in for ancestor worship?

An Old Testament ghost town   (6 mins)

The city stood high in rugged hill country. Below, there was a pass through the hills. But the site itself was surrounded by precipitous gorges. The Old Testament calls the place Ai, but nobody knows what the city was really called. The name Ai means 'the ruin'. It was a ruin in Old Testament times. Only the archaeologists can tell you about Ai. Although the site was occupied for over seven hundred years, we don't know the name of a single person who lived there.

The earliest people lived in a village. In about 3,100 B.C., they inhabited pits dug into the earth at Ai. Many of them were not natives of the Holy Land. People from different places made different types of pottery – and a variety of styles has been found by the archaeologists. The general movement of peoples in those early times was from the north, and Ai received some of the migrants – exactly what one might expect of a village on a pass through the hill country at a time when there were many nomads.

But Ai didn't remain a village for long. A great city was built in about 3,000 B.C. On the highest part of the mound there was an imposing fortified acropolis. Inside there were two important buildings – a large temple and the palace of the king of Ai. Defensive walls were also built around the city at that time, and here and there the military engineers built tall towers. There were four city gates. The pottery tells us that the original villagers continued to live at Ai, but the bold and imaginative planning of the new city shows that a ruler had taken over who knew about urban development. The city was reminiscent of those to be found at the time in northern Syria or Turkey.

Ai was destroyed with great violence in about 2,860 B.C. Scorched stones and a layer of ashes tell of this attack by an unknown enemy. Afterwards, a further new ruler seems to have taken power and the city was rebuilt. Buildings and gateways were modified. The temple was restored and a new royal palace was built – much reduced in size. This third phase came to an end with the total destruction of Ai in an earthquake in about 2,720 B.C. Most of the buildings at that time were made from mud-bricks, likely to crumble very quickly in an earthquake.

Following this destruction, the city was again rebuilt. The archaeologists have detected evidence of Egyptian craftsmanship in the work of this period. Egypt was a great power in the Middle East at that time, and very likely Egyptian troops had taken over the city. The masonry of the rebuilt temple was typical of Egyptian workmanship at the time. The building was plastered and painted with great elegance. At this stage, Ai contained the earliest known city water system in the Holy Land. It was an ingenious piece of careful engineering and again gives evidence of Egyptian expertise.

Ai was seiged and captured in about 2,550 B.C. and from then on the Egyptian influence disappeared. One of the most surprising developments was that the temple at Ai, which had been on the same site since the time of the earliest city, was now re-used as the royal palace. The previous royal buildings had been filled with rubble, perhaps as a result of the attack on the city. The temple was the only usable building on the acropolis, and the king took it for himself. Why is this surprising? To the people of the time, nothing was more important than religion − except perhaps life itself. The ruler of Ai lived in what had been the temple because it was the best fortified building in the city. An Arab workman who helped the archaeologists when they were excavating at Ai summed it up. 'The people who lived here,' he said, 'were frightened.'

The use of the temple as a royal residence, though, did not mean that the people gave up their religion. A new sanctuary was created in a remodelled house nearby. The archaeologists have noticed that the Egyptian-style pottery from the old temple was moved to the new sanctuary. And further vessels, added during this period, were in the style associated with the people of the north of Canaan. But the Egyptians came back. Ai was completely destroyed in about 2,400 B.C., almost certainly by an Egyptian army.

For over a thousand years after that, nobody lived at Ai. Then, in about 1,200 B.C., a tiny village grew on the mound. The ruins of the great fortifications which still stood there were not restored by the newcomers. Their numbers were small and they could not defend such a large site. The new people of Ai were farmers and shepherds. Terracing has been found from this period as well as querns for grinding flour. And we can see the remains of their small, stone-built houses. This village lasted for about a hundred and fifty years before enemies destroyed it. Ai was finally deserted in about 1,050 B.C. perhaps after a fight. Slingstones have been found in the remains of the houses. But the village was left standing after its abandonment. No wonder the Old Testament calls the place Ai − the ruin.

QUESTIONS FOR DEBATE

1. What kinds of remains might the archaeologists of the future find when excavating one of our cities?
2. Why is it likely that the people of the future will know far more about us than we know about the people of the past? (clues: film, television, libraries, newspapers, museums etc.)

Shechem   (6 mins)

The relationship between the Israelites and the Land of Canaan began sometime in the nineteenth century B.C. A great many of the fortified cities of the Holy Land, such as Jericho, were ancient even then — the centres of a well developed Canaanite civilization. Ai was already a ruin.

READER
>And Abram took Sarai his wife, and Lot his brother's son, and all the possessions which they had gathered, and the persons that they had gotten in Haran; and they set forth to go to the land of Canaan. When they came to the land of Canaan, Abram passed through the land to the place at Shechem, to the oak of Moreh. At that time the Canaanites were in the land. Then the Lord appeared to Abram and said, 'To your descendants will I give this land'. So he built there an altar to the Lord, who had appeared to him.

That account of the coming of Abram is to be found in Genesis, chapter 12. He was called Abram at that time — only later did he change his name to Abraham. He came from Haran in the Mesopotamian valley and, like many before him, he was following the general drift of peoples on the move at that time. So many of the new people to arrive in the Land of Canaan came from the countries to the north. Many details are left out of the biblical account. We are not told, for instance, what route he followed on this journey. We are told only that he arrived at a Canaanite city called Shechem and received a vision there in which his God promised him possession of the land.

The lack of detail in the story is not surprising. The biblical account of Abram's arrival was not written down at the time. For centuries, the stories about him were passed on by word of mouth from generation to generation. In this way was knowledge of Abram preserved when his descendants did not read or write. They were keen to remember the information accurately. But the most important aspects of the stories were remembered, while the details were forgotten.

Rediscovering the details is one of the excitements of modern archaeology in the Holy Land. A visit to the site of ancient Shechem brings the story of Abram to life. The city is marked by a high mound at the entrance to a narrow gorge between Mount Gerizim and Mount Ebal in the central spine of the Holy Land. Nowadays, the modern Arab village of El Balatah stands on the southern slope of the mound. The city was heavily fortified long before Abram's time. Thick stone walls and high towers had been built to protect the inhabitants of a city on a pass through the hill country. El Balatah is now a Palestinian refugee camp.

But Shechem was also an important centre of Canaanite religion. The remains of a remarkable courtyard temple have been found, separated from the rest of the city by a stout wall. There were sacrificial altars and, at the centre, was a large, carefully-smoothed stone pillar. It was found lying near the socket into which it fitted. The people of ancient Shechem worshipped fertility gods. They expected the gods to make the land fertile and to help their flocks to prosper. They possessed magical figurines and charms as symbols of their gods.

The importance which this sanctuary gained in Israelite eyes can be shown by gathering information about it later in the Old Testament. We are told that Abram's grandson Jacob buried charms and figurines at the oak tree of Moreh – where Abram built his altar. Later, the bones of his great grandson Joseph were brought back from Egypt to the same place for burial. A domed building on the east slope of Mount Gerizim marks the spot where, according to tradition, Joseph was buried. While archaeology cannot vouch for the story of the arrival of Abram, it helps to make it credible. When people go on pilgrimage, they usually visit holy places. The temple at Shechem in Abram's time was an important shrine. He could build an altar there and, in such a place, he could expect to receive visions.

QUESTIONS FOR DEBATE

1. The earliest phase in the building of Stonehenge was probably started in about 1,800 B.C. We know practically nothing about why it was built. Why do we know so much more about the religion of ancient Canaan?
2. Why did people, before they could read and write, take care to remember stories as accurately as possible?

Abram comes to Shechem   (4 mins)

Progress was slow. Below them, the bed of the river scored its way through a narrow valley between high banks. The nomads and their flocks of sheep and goats were obliged to struggle along rough parched tracks high above the river, looking for a descent to an ancient crossing place. Behind them straggled the pack camels and donkeys. This was the Jordan. In the distance beyond the river hung the twin mountain peaks of Ebal and Gerizim — a precipitous ascent to the west of three thousand feet in nine miles! That hill country was the destination of these travellers, offering better pasture for the flocks. At last they came to the ford at Adam — famous for landslides which could block the river. The bleating flock jostled awkwardly through the waters. In the evening, they moved slowly into the base of the Wadi Fari'a — a narrow, wandering gorge rising gently towards the hills.

This was a land of dramatic contrasts. The wadi had steep barren sides. Yet at the base of the gorge, the porous rocks of the mountain range supplied a multitude of small springs to water the tall trees and rich meadows. Towards dusk, their black, goat hair tents were pitched in the fertile base of the wadi. Abram, leader of this expedition, contemplated the scenery. His nephew Lot played a little haunting tune on a pipe. It was a satisfying moment at the end of the long day. The menservants were watering the flocks at a small spring. Abram looked over at Sarai his wife and the rest of the women as they struggled with heavy stones and boulders to make a rough enclosure for the sheep. The goats were not to be penned — because they were much less valuable than the sheep. As the women worked, Abram had time for thought.

This journey was his pilgrimage. Abram believed that he had been divinely called to leave his home at Haran in the north country. He believed too that he was now expected to dwell in the land into which his God would lead him. With Sarai his wife, Lot his nephew, his servants and his flocks he had entered this land. He saw it as the beginning of a new life and every step brought it nearer. This was not simply a journey. It was also a pilgrimage for his God.

The following day, Abram and his retinue set off once more. In the late afternoon, the wadi led them to the great Canaanite city called Shechem. There were soldiers on the massive walls of the city and guards stood at the gates. Yet the sight of a wandering shepherd and his goods did not trouble the Shechemites. The nomads were allowed to pitch their tents on some higher ground opposite one of the city gates. Then Abram entered Shechem and visited the great temple sanctuary within the city. It was a place where men worshipped their gods.

Afterwards, outside the city, Abram found a grove of oak trees. There he built an altar and, in the cool of the evening, he made a sacrifice to his God. But this shepherd of ancient times, famous in the pages of the Bible, did not stay near Shechem. The following day, he moved on deeper into the land which he had been promised. He camped that night with the great Canaanite city of Bethel to the west and the ghost town called Ai to the east.

QUESTIONS FOR DEBATE

1. What does the story tell you about the attitude towards women among the members of these nomadic tribes?
2. What information had been added to the biblical story in order to prepare this account?

The Kings' highway   (6 mins)

A road ran almost directly south in ancient times from the Mesopotamian valley down to the Gulf of Aqaba. In most places it was only a rough track and, in places, it involved negotiating high mountain passes. But this was one of the great trade routes of the ancient Middle East. Merchants, with their strings of pack-camels or donkeys, transported silk and spices, copper and pottery to sell to the cities on the way. Some of the merchandise reached the trading ships which plied from Aqaba visiting the ports of the African and Arabian coasts. In less peaceful times, the road was also used by warring armies. Sometime around 1,800 B.C., Amraphel king of Shinar, Arioch king of Ellasar, Chedorlaomer king of Elam and Tidal king of Goiim made a military excursion along that road. These were kings who ruled cities in the northern part of the Mesopotamian valley.

The expedition led to great violence as the four kings subdued the cities on the way. Probably none of them could have made the journey alone, but their combined armies made a formidable force. When they got to Aqaba, they turned north and headed into the Negev — the desert in the south of the Land of Canaan. There they took the city of Kadesh-barnea. Then they turned eastwards again, and descended into the valley of the Dead Sea. This excursion had two purposes. Conquered cities could be forced to pay tribute. But the kings also wanted bitumen from the Dead Sea to caulk their ships at Tyre, the busiest seaport of the ancient world.

The Dead Sea is one of the strangest stretches of water on earth. It lies a thousand feet below sea level, a complex mixture of chemicals. There are salt-encrusted rocks and viscous waters, great sulphurous bays and, in places, salt floes emerging from the surface. The desert valley in which the Dead Sea lies is sterilized of life by the minerals. But the kings did not obtain their bitumen from the Dead Sea without opposition. Five local Canaanite kings took their armies against them in battle. These were the kings of Sodom, Gomorrah, Admah, Zeboim and Bela. We don't know where any of those cities were situated. But the marauding kings of the north defeated the local kings and many of the Canaanite soldiers perished in the waters of the Dead Sea.

Taking the bitumen and some prisoners with them the kings then headed triumphantly for home. The Bible tells the story because biblical characters became involved at this point. Lot and his family were among the prisoners taken by the kings. Lot was Abram's nephew and lived at this time in Sodom. Abram himself had settled at Mamre in the Judean hill country. A Canaanite soldier fleeing from the battle told him what had happened. The Bible then gives us what seems surprising information about Abram:

READER

> When Abram heard that his kinsman had been taken captive, he led forth his trained men, born in his house, three hundred and eighteen of them . . .

The usual impression given in Genesis is that Abram was a shepherd leader of a small company of nomads. But here the picture is different. According to this, Abram and his kinsman were sufficient in number to take on the marauding kings. He led his men to the Upper Jordan Valley north of the Sea of Galilee and attacked the invaders by night. The kings of the north and their armies were put to flight, and Lot and his family were rescued.

This story about the journey of the kings and their defeat by Abram is told in Genesis, chapter 14. Many scholars think that it was written a great deal earlier than any of the other stories about Abram. Most of the stories about him were passed on by word of mouth for many centuries before they were written down. Consequently, the most important events were remembered, but often the details of a story were forgotten. But this is detailed history. And there is another interesting piece of information. From that time onwards, the road which the kings first took from the Mesopotamian valley to the Gulf of Aqaba became known as the 'Kings' Highway'.

QUESTIONS FOR DEBATE

1. Why do you think the details of a story were better preserved when they were written down?
2. Can you suggest reasons why a piece of history about the defeat of marauding kings was written down earlier than the other stories about Abram?

Ancient Accho   (5 mins)

Accho was the original name of the city. The ancient site lies in a flat, fertile plain about a mile inland from the sea. On the coast is one of the few natural harbours of the Holy Land. The coast of the Holy Land is very regular and affords few harbours. But, in the north, the western end of the Carmel Range forms a pro- monotary called the Antelope's Nose. Beyond is a wide bay in which the harbour lies.

The harbour is the clue to the existence of this ancient city. The caravan route from Damascus and the east — really not much more than an ancient beaten track — arrived at the Mediterranean coast here. In the nineteenth century B.C. and probably much earlier, merchants moved to and fro along that route buying in one market and selling in another. Goods travelled astonishing distances — to far- away India in the east and to the countries of Europe in the west. The market at ancient Accho was an important staging post in the flow of that trade. Probably people of many origins lived there, but Accho was essentially a Phoenecian city. The Phoenecians were the busiest sea-trading people of the ancient world and their cities also flourished along the coast of the Lebanon to the north.

The earliest written reference to the harbour appears in Egyptian records. Egypt at the time was the most powerful kingdom in the Middle East. Cities were cap- tured by the Egyptians and tribute was exacted. The Pharoah Pepi 1 made a series of campaigns into the Holy Land in about 2,350 B.C. In one of them, Pepi sent two forces simultaneously — one by sea and the other by land — into the country he called 'The land of the sand dwellers'. His naval force is described as landing behind the 'nose of the Antelope's Head' — clearly the harbour at Accho, although there is no mention of the city itself in these Egyptian records.

About five hundred years later, towards the end of the nineteenth century B.C., many of the cities of the Holy Land were in rebellion against Egyptian power. The Egyptians, in a rather unusual fashion, have supplied us with a record of the names of the rulers of these rebel cities. Little clay figures in human form were made. On each of them was inscribed the name of an enemy of Egypt, together with curses on him. These cursing vessels — we call them Execration Texts — were then smashed to show what Egypt would do to such an enemy. The remains of many of these smashed vessels have survived including the one promising destruc- tion to Accho. It tells us that the rebellious ruler of the city at the time was a man called Taram.

The mound on which ancient Accho stood can be seen alongside the road which today enters the modern city. It is a steep-sided accumulation of earth and debris, built up by a multitude of generations and rising to a height of about eighty feet. Near bedrock level, the archaeologists have excavated a well-preserved gateway from the nineteenth century B.C. — about the time when the Egyptians were making their Execration Texts. The gateway is built of mud-brick and its design is ingenious. It contains two inner guard rooms and three successive doorways, each of which could be defended in turn. Clearly, in the nineteenth century B.C., Accho was a well-built and well-fortified city.

A great deal of the mound of ancient Accho is still unexcavated. The visitor may well wonder what else will be found in the future. The ancient gateway is the most exciting archaeological discovery made so far. Defended by such a gateway, Accho was clearly a prosperous place. Within the walls of the city, there must have been streets, temples, public buildings and, of course, a busy market place. Probably about 3,000 inhabitants lived there in small mud-brick houses.

Many of the people of ancient Accho worked in the market, or manned the port. Mariners from the city sailed the flimsy Phoenecian ships the length and the breadth of the Mediterranean Sea. Others inhabitants developed agriculture in the fertile plain which surrounds the city. Such people returned every night to safety within the walls of Accho. There were no farmsteads in the countryside of the Holy Land at that time. Enemies abounded, and people were obliged to live in properly fortified cities. Although this was an important city of the Holy Land, the Old Testament mentions Accho only once and adds practically nothing to our information. Abraham, the founding father of the Israelites, lived in the Holy Land in the nineteenth century B.C. But in the centuries that followed, his descendants became slaves in Egypt. The Israelites did not return until sometime in the thirteenth century B.C., after their escape from Egypt and after long wanderings in the desert. They found it easy to penetrate the Holy Land because large areas of the countryside were not defended. On their arrival, the Israelites divided up the Holy Land among the twelve tribes. Accho was within the territory allocated to the tribe of Asher. But in the Book of the Judges there is a complaint that the tribe did not conquer Accho. It was not unusual at the time for the incoming Israelites to fail to take such a strong, fortified city as this.

QUESTIONS FOR DEBATE

1. Why do you think archaeological excavation is such a slow process?
2. Do you think the Egyptian Execration Texts had a religious significance?

The Israelites

The coming of the Israelites   (5 mins)

After their escape from slavery in Egypt, the Israelite tribes wandered the great
empty spaces of the Sinai wilderness. This was a stark and barren land. Sinai,
craggy and mountainous, provided breathtaking scenery, the arid stretches of the
red sandstone plains dominated by the dark granite of the extensive mountain ranges.
Yet everywhere there were unexpected contrasts. Hidden within this landscape
were luxuriant and well-watered valleys, and terraced hillsides covered in olives.
It was not all barren. But nothing was on a small scale.

For the most part, the Israelites lived like the Bedouin tribes of today, their flocks
of sheep and goats wresting a meagre living out of the rugged land. The tribes
were widely scattered in this difficult terrain, their tribal leaders deciding when
and where to move in search of new pasture. Yet contacts were maintained with
the other tribes, and there was a clearly-defined social order among them. Moses,
who had led the nation out of Egypt, was their recognized chief.

During their years in the desert, each day brought its own labours, its own hardships, for the Israelites. If they planted crops during the rainy winter months, only
rarely did they see a harvest. Usually the hot sun of early spring destroyed the
young plants before they could bear fruit. Yet the attempt was made year after
year. Only once in about every five years did they succeed. When a crop failed,
the tribes moved on, in search of the sparse grass which would keep their sheep
and goats alive.

Unlike the Bedouin tribes of today, the Israelites had not chosen this desert
existence. It had been forced upon them by circumstances. When they had escaped
from the power of the Egyptians, they were faced on all sides by enemies — too
weak a nation to face armed conflict. The desert was the only place into which
they could go to survive.

These were among the poorest people on the face of the earth. Yet during their
sojourn in the desert, the Israelites considered themselves the most fortunate of
people. They believed that the God of Israel had brought them out of Egypt by

the hand of their leader Moses — that their God had saved them from many and great dangers. He had fed them in the wilderness and had found water for them in the desert rocks. During this time of wandering and poverty, the children of Israel were gradually welded into a nation and into a religion. And, at Mount Sinai itself, they believed that their God had given them even greater gifts:

READER

  I am the Lord your God, who brought you out of the land of Egypt, out of the house of bondage.

  You shall have no other gods before me.

So reads the first of the Ten Commandments, which Moses received on Mount Sinai. These were the laws by which they should live. And during the time in the desert, the Israelites had a single purpose. They believed that, centuries before, the God of Israel had promised the Land of Canaan to their ancestor Abraham. The purpose of their pilgrimage through the desert was to lead them to the land promised to their forefathers.

The first Canaanite city which the Israelites took as they came into the Land of Canaan was Jericho. According to the Old Testament, the walls of the city miraculously fell down to let the Israelites in. Kathleen Kenyon, the famous British archaeologist, has excavated the site of ancient Jericho. While the Jordan valley is dry most of the year, it rains heavily in the winter months. Over the centuries, the evidence as to what happened when the Israelites came has been washed away in these rains. We cannot prove the Bible story from the archaeology. Yet the Jordan valley is prone to earthquakes, and the walls of the city at that time were built of mud-brick, liable to crumble if an earthquake took place.

QUESTIONS FOR DEBATE

1. Why do you think that religious beliefs were important to these people during their time in the desert?
2. Why can the beginning of law be regarded as a step forward in the development of civilization?

Lachish   (7 mins)

The site of the ancient city of Lachish stands west of Jerusalem, where the hills of the central spine of the Holy Land descend to the flat coastal plain of the Mediterranean seaboard. In ancient times, a road ran from the north and passed near Lachish, hugging the foothills on one side and skirting the plain on the other. This was called the 'Way of the Sea', but the road was not near the sea at this point because the coastal plain was a mosquito-ridden swamp. The 'Way of the Sea' was the international road, running south from Damascus in the direction of Egypt. It was used particularly by traders and by warring armies. The Holy Land was a corridor between the great powers, and there was nearly always a war.

Anyone visiting the site of Lachish today will see a mound about seventy feet high rising above the surrounding countryside. The original city was first built on this mound, but it was not nearly as high in the early days. The Canaanites who lived there between about four and five thousand years ago, chose the site because it was easier to defend than lower-lying ground. Egypt was the most powerful country in the world at the time, and the Canaanites knew that they needed strong fortifications.

Generation after generation lived at Lachish. The ordinary people inhabited small, single-roomed houses made of mud-brick. Because the weather in the Land of Canaan was usually warm and sunny, most of their lives were spent out of doors. They only went inside to sleep and to eat. Over the centuries, as older houses were demolished and new ones were built, the mound became higher and higher. Lachish, as one sees it now, is really the remains of a vast, historic human ant-heap. In the thirteenth century B.C., when the Israelites were wandering tribes in the Sinai desert, Lachish was already a city well over a thousand years old. It was one of the Canaanite cities which the Israelites took soon after their arrival. From then on, Lachish was an Israelite city, but there were probably many Canaanites living there as well.

Let's picture the city in its heyday. Small round stones had been dug into the sides of the mound and covered with a layer of plaster, making the sides of the mound very slippery. Above this 'glacis', thick walls had been built all round the city, wide enough at the top to take a great many defenders. There were also towers at various points in the walls. The defenders always had the advantage of height over an enemy. The road up to the gateway of Lachish curved up from the right. It meant that troops approaching the gate were exposed to the bowmen on the walls. A soldier wore his shield on his left arm, and the road had been placed so that a man's right side was exposed to the defenders. The people who designed these fortifications were particularly anxious about the gate — the weakest point in their defences.

The way armies went about laying seige to such a city as Lachish in Old Testament times is described by Sennacherib, King of Assyria in the eighth century B.C. It is inscribed on a clay tablet found in the remains of his palace in Assyria. At that time, Hezekiah was King of Judah, and Lachish was one of his cities:

READER

But as for Hezekiah, the Jew who did not bow in submission to my yoke, forty-six of his strong walled towns and innumerable small villages in their neighbourhood I beseiged and conquered by stamping down earth ramps, and then bringing up battering rams, by the assault of foot soldiers, by breaches, tunnelling and sapper operations.

Sennacherib went about it quite ruthlessly. The remains of the gigantic ramp which his troops built to take the city can still be seen at Lachish. Tons and tons of rubble were piled up against the sides of the mound by Assyrian troops, while the defenders poured arrows and slingstones into their midst. Those ancient wars involved human death on a vast scale.

The archaeologists have excavated much of the mound at Lachish. Many interesting objects from the past have been found — mirrors from Egypt, Philistine pottery, the remains of ancient games. But one of the most interesting finds is a series of letters discovered in the remains of the gateway. They are written in ink on bits of unglazed pottery, and are addressed to the commander at Lachish in 587 B.C. At that time, a Babylonian army was invading the Holy Land — along the 'Way of the Sea'. The Babylonians worked their way along that road, sieging one city after another. The nearest city to Lachish was called Azekah.

To be informed about the progress of the Babylonian army, the commander at Lachish had sent a small troop of Israelite spies up into the hills. Each night, the cities which had not been taken lit beacons. When a beacon was not lit, they knew that that city had fallen. The Lachish letters, as they are called, are reports to the commander. The terse wording of the last of the letters emphasizes the tension as Azekah fails to light a beacon:

READER

. . . we are watching the signal-stations of
Lachish, according to all the signs which my
Lord gives, because we do not see the signals
of Azekah . . .

The Babylonians have nearly arrived.

The story of the Old Testament is a story of war. In ancient times the Holy Land was one of the most dangerous places in the world in which to live. But remarkably, out of the centuries of human suffering came a great collection of religious writings. We find them in the Bible. It is impossible to explain in purely rational terms why that country became a source of religious belief. But it does seem that out of centuries of human suffering there came also a profound perception of God.

QUESTIONS FOR DEBATE

1. Which world religions are associated with the Holy Land?
2. Do you think there is a connexion between human suffering and religion?

Jebus   (4 mins)

The ancient city of Jebus stood on a high ridge in a remote part of the Holy Land. To the east, at the bottom of a deep valley ran a small stream called the Gihon. It was the only source of water available to the earliest inhabitants of Jebus. The city walls were built high on the sides of the ridge and, within the walls, there was a central fortress. Armed men, stout walls and strong fortifications on a ridge were formidable obstacles to an enemy. But the Jebusites, as the inhabitants were called, were obliged to come out of the city walls to collect water from the Gihon. The city would fall to a siege lasting only a short time — because there was no water supply within the city.

We don't know how early in their history the problem was solved by the Jebusites. But the archaeologists have found the remains of their water system. A shaft was cut through the rock from within the walls of Jebus. The upper part of that shaft was a long tunnel in which steps descended. Then, at the end, there was a vertical shaft falling to a tunnel which brought water under the city from the Gihon in the valley below. People could descend the stepped corridor and lower their leather buckets down the shaft into the tunnel. From then on the Jebusites could collect water without going outside the city walls. The original work of creating the shaft must have taken a great deal of labour. It involved cutting through the rock to a depth of over seventy feet. Yet it is clear that the scheme gave the Jebusites a great feeling of security within their fortifications. The Old Testament makes what appears at first to be a mysterious reference to the defences of the city of Jebus:

READER

> And the king and his men went against the Jebusites, the inhabitants of the land, who said to David, 'You shall not come in here but the blind and the lame will ward you off' . . .

To understand it, we must remember what was happening at the time. The Israelites had come into the Land of Canaan some two centuries earlier. By this time, they were led by King David, the most able military commander in their history. City after city had fallen into his hands. Yet the defences of Jebus were so formidable that the Jebusites felt able to make a joke. They said that the place could be defended by a troop of blind and lame soldiers. But the Old Testament also tells us how David responded:

READER

> And David said on that day, 'Whoever would smite the Jebusites, let him get up the water shaft to attack the lame and the blind who are hated by David's soul'.

Probably by night, a gang of armed Israelites waded into the tunnel. One of their number struggled the thirty-five or so feet up the vertical part of the shaft. Then he let down a rope. Once these men were inside, they could attack the guards on the city gates and let in the rest of David's army. The city of Jebus had fallen:

READER

> And David dwelt in the stronghold, and called it the city of David.

There was, though, another ancient name for this city. It was also Urusalim – the city of peace. To this day the city of David, captured from the Jebusites by sending men through the water shaft, is called Jerusalem.

QUESTIONS FOR DEBATE

1. Many of the cities of the Holy Land were built on the international route called the 'Way of the Sea'. But why do you think it was important that Jerusalem, the holy city, should be out of the way?
2. Do you think Jerusalem – the 'city of peace' – is an apt name for the city?

Araunah the Jebusite   (6 mins)

There has always been a strong connexion between food and religion. Whenever harvests have been plentiful, many people have felt the need to thank God for his gifts. And they have also prayed to God in time of famine. In ancient Israel, the harvesting of corn took place in the early summer. The harvesters used sickles to cut the fields of corn in the valleys. Then they took the stalks, heavy with grain, to the threshing floor.

In about 1,000 B.C., nearly three thousand years ago, there was a threshing floor on a high ridge near the city of Jerusalem. It belonged to a man called Araunah the Jebusite. Before the city had been captured by King David, Jerusalem had belonged to his people and had been called Jebus. In the early summer, Araunah and his men could be seen struggling up to the threshing floor, his oxen pulling the small wooden carts laden with corn. The threshing floor itself was marked by a circle of stones into which they unloaded the carts.

When this was done, Araunah's men hitched the oxen to heavy wooden sledges. Inset into each sledge were a series of sharp edged flint stones. The oxen pulled the sledges round and round within the threshing floor. The flints cut up the stalks of corn into short lengths and loosened the grains. Then the men took flat wooden forks and tossed the mixture of grain and chaff into the air. The wind on the ridge blew the chaff away, but the grains of corn fell back into the stone circle. It was a neat way of separating the grain from the chaff. The threshing floor was on a high ridge because there was more wind up there.

In Araunah's time, there was a holy man called Gad who acted as adviser to King David. David was the greatest king in the history of Israel. He had conquered Israel's enemies and had given the nation a long period of peace. But there came a time when the city of Jerusalem was in serious trouble. Many people were dying of the plague. It was Gad who thought of a way of resolving the problem. In those days, people believed that God would help them if they offered sacrifices to him. It's worth reading the part of the Bible which tells us of Gad's advice and what happened next:

READER
> And Gad came that day to David, and said to him,
> 'Go up, rear an altar to the Lord on the threshing
> floor of Araunah the Jebusite.' So David went up.
> And Araunah said, 'Why has my lord come to his
> servant?' David said, 'To buy the threshing floor
> of you, in order to build an altar to the Lord,
> that the plague may be averted from my people.'

Then Araunah said to David, 'Let my lord the king
take and offer up what seems good to him; here are
the oxen for the burnt offering, and the threshing
sledges and the yokes of the oxen for the wood. All
this, O king, Araunah gives to the king.' But the
king said to Araunah, 'No but I will buy it of you
for a price; I will not offer burnt offerings to
the Lord which cost me nothing.' So David bought
the threshing floor and the oxen for fifty sheckels
of silver. And David built there an altar to the
Lord, and offered burnt offerings and peace
offerings. So the Lord heeded supplications for the
land, and the plague was averted from Israel.

The threshing floor, where King David built an altar for his sacrifice, became
in the following reign the site of the Temple, the holiest place in Israel. King David
bought it in the first place because his people were suffering from the plague. But
the site was chosen because it was a threshing floor. Bread was regarded by the
people of ancient Israel as God's greatest gift to mankind.

QUESTIONS FOR DEBATE

1. Why do you think it was important to King David that he paid for Araunah's
threshing floor?
2. Why do you think that so many of the world religions express themselves in
terms of food?

The divided kingdom   (4 mins)

After King David's death, his son Solomon came to the throne. King Solomon
was responsible for building the magnificent Temple on the ridge above the city
of Jerusalem. The altar which his father David had set up on the threshing floor

of Araunah the Jebusite became the holiest place in the land. Solomon also fortified many of the great cities of the Holy Land. Such building schemes, though,
cost a great deal of money and heavy taxes were exacted from the people in the
north of his kingdom. But Solomon did not tax the people in the south, near his
capital city Jerusalem.

After Solomon's death, there was a revolt against his son Rehoboam. The people of the north were afraid of even heavier taxes. As a result, the nation was
divided into two new kingdoms — called Israel in the north, and Judah in the south.
Jeroboam, the son of Nebat, led the revolt of the people of the north and became
the first king of the new kingdom of Israel. But the Old Testament is very critical
of the reign of Jeroboam. It says that he made Israel to sin because he encouraged
people to worship other gods instead of the God of the Israelites.

There were good reasons why Jeroboam encouraged the people of his kingdom
to worship the local gods. He did not want his subjects to go to the Temple in
Jerusalem. The Holy City was in the kingdom of Judah and ruled by Rehoboam.
The two kingdoms were often at war. For that reason, Jeroboam encouraged the
worship of the Baals — the gods of the Canaanites. By the standards of the time
this was not a particularly terrible thing to do. The Israelites were at that time
quite tolerant of other religions. It was only later, when the history books came
to be written, that the worship of other gods was regarded with abhorrence. The
history writers of the Old Testament — like many other historians since — read
their own values into history. The judgements of the historians are to be seen over
and over again in the biblical accounts of this period. In the mid-ninth century
B.C., for instance, the kingdom of Israel had a very competent king on the throne.
His name was Ahab. The capital of Israel when he came to the throne was Tirzah,
at the head of the Wadi Faria — the deep narrow valley famous because Abraham
had come to the Promised Land that way. The city stood high above the valley,
but it was likely to be attacked in time of war because it was on one of the routes
which led into the hill country. One of the first things Ahab did was to establish
a new capital at Samaria — a much less vulnerable position for a capital city.

His reign, as with most of the reigns of the kings of Israel and Judah, was a
period of successive wars. Ahab won most of them. His most important conflict
was with Ben-Hadad, king of Damascus. Ben Hadad came and besieged Samaria
— but was beaten off by Ahab. The Syrian commanders blamed the hills surrounding Samaria for their defeat:

READER

> Their gods are the gods of the hills, and so they were stronger than
> we, but let us fight against them in the plain, and surely we shall be
> stronger than they.

It was typical superstitious thinking of the time. Ahab gave the lie to it by taking his army up onto the Golan heights — a flat and open plain. He engaged the Syrians in a pitched battle at Aphek and roundly defeated them again. But Ahab, according to the history books of the Old Testament, was a bad king:

READER
> And Ahab, the son of Omri, did evil in the sight of the Lord more than all that were before him.

And the reason? He was married to Jezebel, the daughter of the Phoenecian king of Tyre. And he had built a temple to the Phoenecian god Melcart for his wife Jezebel. The people of the time saw little wrong in it, but to the biblical historians it was indeed evil.

QUESTIONS FOR DEBATE

1. Is it possible to have sympathy with the biblical historians?
2. Is it possible to have sympathy with the superstition of the Syrian commanders?

Elijah the Tishbite   (5 mins)

Elijah the Tishbite was the first prophet to condemn the idea that other gods could be worshipped in Israel. For him only the God of Israel mattered. Elijah lived at the time of Ahab in the mid-ninth century B.C., and caused the king of Israel many problems. Yet the stories we have about the prophet are intriguing. Some of them are obviously legend, while others are equally clearly based on fact.

   The first story about Elijah in the Old Testament comes during a period of drought. We find him on the banks of the brook Cherith, east of the River Jordan. The writers of the history books of the Old Testament almost certainly started with this story because they wanted to establish Elijah as a man of God, to whom miraculous things would happen. They say that on the banks of the Cherith, Elijah was fed by the ravens. Later in the same story, we hear that the prophet has moved to Zarephath in Galilee, and is living with a widow and her son. Miraculously, the little food and olive oil which the widow had stored did not run out during the whole period of the drought and the famine that went with it. Towards the end of this first story, Elijah seems to have done mouth to mouth resuscitation on her son. If so, he was many centuries ahead of his time.

In the second story about Elijah, there is the first open confrontation with Ahab. According to the history books, Jezebel had ordered the killing of the prophets of the Lord. But Obadiah, Ahab's chief minister, had hidden a hundred prophets in a cave. Elijah appeared dramatically before Obadiah, and demanded to see Ahab. Obadiah was frightened at the thought of it:

READER
> As soon as I have gone from you, the spirit of the Lord will carry you whither I know not; and so, when I come and tell Ahab and he cannot find you, he will kill me.

It was only when Elijah had solemnly promised to stay where he was that Obadiah went off to find Ahab. Ahab came face to face with Elijah:

READER
> Is it you, you troubler of Israel? And he answered, 'I have not troubled Israel, but you have, and your father's house, because you have forsaken the commandments of the Lord and followed the Baals.'

It proves Elijah's courage in taking on the king, and the fear which Ahab felt when facing him.

The encounter led to a great contest between the prophets of Baal and Elijah on the top of Mount Carmel. Both the Baal prophets and Elijah built altars of sacrifice. But fire from heaven to light their sacrifice did not come for the Baal prophets. Only Elijah was able to do that. Was it a thunderbolt? We don't know. The Elijah stories are rather like the James Bond stories — just this side of the possible. At the end of this story, Elijah incited the crowd to kill the Baal prophets. And there was heavy rain. The drought was ended.

In the third story, Elijah was very dejected. He felt as though Jezebel would succeed in defeating his purposes. He wanted to die in the desert, but was fed by angels and led to make a long journey to Mount Sinai — the mountain from which the Israelites received the Ten Commandments. This is the most atmospheric and the most spiritual of the Elijah stories. On the mountain, Elijah hid in a cave. He experienced electric storms, earthquakes, fires and tempests. But he heard the voice of God as a still, small voice after the storms were over. God commissioned him to anoint new kings over Damascus and Israel.

In the next story, Ahab is again shown in a bad light. An ordinary man called Naboth had a vineyard which Ahab desired. According to the Old Testament, Jezebel had him stoned to death. She then gave the vineyard to Ahab. This resulted in a fierce encounter between Ahab and Elijah. It led, in due course, to the death of Jezebel − thrown to the dogs from a tower at Samaria. But the judgement of the historians is suspect. Reading between the lines, Jezebel was a proud and sophisticated woman. She put on all her make up and finery, knowing that she was going to be killed by an unruly gang of yokels, and went out to meet them.

QUESTIONS FOR DEBATE

1. Which parts of the story of Elijah do think are fact, and which parts do you think are legend?
2. Do you think the fact that Elijah had all the prophets of Baal killed after the contest in Mount Carmel puts him in a bad light? Why do you think he did it?

Psalm 23   (9 mins)

READER
          The Lord is my shepherd: therefore can I lack nothing.

So begins the most famous English version of the most famous of all the psalms. The psalms are the poems of the Old Testament, but notice how Hebrew poetry was in a different form from English poetry:

READER

    The Lord's my shepherd, I'll not want;
    He makes me down to lie
    In pastures green; he leadeth me
       The quiet waters by.

That's how the same psalm has been translated into the style in which much English poetry is written — utilizing rhythm and rhyme. But Hebrew poetry did not use such devices. It was instead a matter of balance — two balancing parts of a line arising out of the same basic idea:

READER

    The Lord is my shepherd: therefore can I lack nothing. It means God is my protector — nothing can go wrong.

The comparison of God to a shepherd is typical of the Old Testament. Shepherds played an important part in the early stories of the Israelites. The patriarchs Abraham and his son Isaac were shepherds. So was Jacob who was next in succession — the man who took the name 'Israel', so that his descendants became known as 'the children of Israel'. Later, Moses, who brought the Israelites out of the land of Egypt and at whose hand they received the law, also spent some time working as a shepherd. And David was the greatest king Israel ever had. Yet when he destroyed the Philistine champion Goliath of Gath, he was merely a shepherd boy.

    There is a great deal of talk in the Bible about good shepherds and bad shepherds. A good shepherd protected his flock from wild beasts, and made sure that they found pasture and water. In this country, one sometimes sees a shepherd, with the help of his sheepdogs, driving his flock along a country road. But it would have been unusual to see a biblical shepherd driving his sheep. A shepherd in the Holy Land led. The flock followed. The sheep and the goats knew that pasture and water would be found for them by the shepherd.

READER

    He shall feed me in a green pasture: and lead me forth beside the waters of comfort.

In the hot summer months, when the shepherds of the Old Testament led their flocks in dry, waterless desert, it took great skill to find pasture and water for the animals. The line tells us how greatly the psalmist appreciates God's skill as his leader.

The psalmist now changes the tone of his poem. God is much more than a skilful shepherd. God is also supremely good:

READER

He shall convert my soul: and bring me forth in the paths of righteousness, for his Name's sake.

If the psalmist follows God, then his life will be full of goodness and truth. Even in the greatest crisis, God is there:

READER

Yea, though I walk through the valley of the shadow of death, I will fear no evil: for thou art with me, thy rod and thy staff comfort me.

Notice the change in the relationship between the psalmist and God as the poem develops. At the beginning, God leads the psalmist just as a Middle Eastern shepherd leads his flock. But in time of trouble, the psalmist has God at his side just as a shepherd will tend to a particular sheep when something has gone wrong.

READER

Thou has prepared a table before me against them that trouble me: thou hast anointed my head with oil, and my cup shall be full.

Just as the shepherd both wards off the enemies of the sheep and supplies his flock with pasture and water, so does God sustain the people who are faithful to him.

READER

But thy loving kindness and mercy shall follow me all the days of my life: and I will dwell in the house of the Lord for ever.

The final promise of the psalm completes the pattern. At the beginning, God leads the psalmist just as the shepherd leads his flock. Later, in time of trouble, God is alongside the psalmist just as a shepherd is with his sheep when things go wrong. Finally, God's loving kindness and mercy follows the psalmist just as a shepherd sometimes follows his flock of sheep.

In many ways, the psalms sum up the Old Testament. In the books of the law and the teachings of the prophets, the religion of the Israelites is shown emerging from their experiences in history. But in the psalms, that experience is brought to life as poets meditate on the relationship between human beings and their God.

QUESTIONS FOR DEBATE

1. In what ways did the religion of Israel develop as a result of its history?
2. Instead of saying 'we have erred and strayed like lost sheep', an Eskimo prayer says 'we have erred and strayed like silly walruses'. Why would the Eskimos find Psalm 23 difficult to understand?

The Greeks

Athena   (5 mins)

High above the modern city of Athens, with its crowded and busy streets, stands the majestic rock of the Acropolis. A passer-by, walking along the broad street below, can look up at the remains of temples built in the Golden Age of classical Greece. These are ruins from the fifth century B.C., the age of Pericles and of the earliest experiment in democracy. Everybody in ancient Athens had a say in the way the city was run — the cobblers and sausage-makers as well as the philosophers and politicians.

Athens is not too far from the sea and the port of the Piraeus. Yet the Acropolis rises to nearly five hundred feet above sea level. The temples in their heyday were the finest built in the ancient world. There was the Erectheion, an elegant building dedicated to the city gods, and the most famous temple of them all — the Parthenon. This was the temple of the maidens, dedicated to the goddess Athena. She gave her name to the city. The tall, slender columns reached up to an elegant pediment. A great frieze ran around. The gods, the goddesses, the demi-gods, the heroes, the youths and the maidens were shown in a great procession — and that on the happiest of all occasions, the festival of the Pananthenaia celebrating the city.

But to understand the Acropolis, it's necessary to think of a time long before the Parthenon was built. The first city stood on the top of this high rock. There were good reasons for it. In ancient times, there were many small local wars. Anyone building a city at ground level was asking for trouble. Enemies would come; the place would be quickly destroyed. But the high rock of the Acropolis could easily be defended. A few soldiers could hold off an army. It explains why so many ancient cities were built on the tops of rocks. In the Holy Land, Jerusalem was built on a high ridge for exactly the same reason.

But the Acropolis had one great advantage over the city of Jerusalem. In Jerusalem, people had to descend from the city to collect water from a little stream which ran in the valley below. But at the northwestern corner of the rock of the

Acropolis, a spring of clear water gushed out of a little crevice. Provided people kept a good store of food in the city, the place could be defended for months. And, in times of peace, it was possible to grow food on the rich plains below the city. One can imagine the people of the time looking down at the sun-drenched land, watching the ripening of the olive trees. The olives were so useful. Not only could the fruit be eaten, but it also provided oil for a multitude of purposes.

Athens was dedicated to two divinities − Athena, the goddess of the olive tree, and Poseidon, the god of the water-spring. Olives and water were the primary possessions of the Athenians. And when the city grew and expanded in the plain below, they developed the site of their original city as a magnificent centre of their religion.

There are many fine statues in the museum at the top of the Acropolis. One of most interesting is the sculpture of a man called Rhombos. It was sculpted in about 570 B.C. It shows us a man wearing a loAcropolis, a spring of clear water gushed out of a little crevice. Provided people kept a good store of food in the city, the place could be defended for months. And, in times of peace, it was possible to grow food on the rich plains below the city. One can imagine the people of the time looking down at the sun-drenched land, watching the ripening of the olive trees. The olives were so useful. Not only could the fruit be eaten, but it also provided oil for a multitude of purposes.

Athens was dedicated to two divinities − Athena, the goddess of the olive tree, and Poseidon, the god of the water-spring. Olives and water were the primary possessions of the Athenians. And when the city grew and expanded in the plain below, they developed the site of their original city as a magnificent centre of their religion.

There are many fine statues in the museum at the top of the Acropolis. One of most interesting is the sculpture of a man called Rhombos. It was sculpted in about 570 B.C. It shows us a man wearing a long tunic, a little round cap on his head. He has a neatly-trimmed beard and is obviously looking his best. Around his shoulders, there is a young calf. Rhombos is holding the animal by the legs. The reason he is looking his best is because he is about to sacrifice the calf to the goddess Athena.

The gods and goddesses of ancient Greece were understood quite differently from the way in which the Israelites understood their God. In the Old Testament, there was only one God whom the Israelites were expected to worship all the days of their lives. They were his 'chosen people'. But the Athenians had many gods and goddesses. They thought of them as superhuman beings − able to do everything which men and women could do, but to perfection. When Rhombos was making his sacrifice to Athena, what he was really doing was celebrating the sheer power of the human spirit. After the sacrifice, he and his friends enjoyed eating the veal. Most of the time, the Athenians got on with their own lives and did not worry about the gods and goddesses. But now and again, sacrifices were made and rituals were observed so that the Greeks could stay on the right side of the gods — could receive their favour. That is exactly what Rhombos was preparing to do when he was sculpted.

QUESTIONS FOR DEBATE

1. In what ways do you think the religion of the Greeks and that of the Israelites was different?
2. Why do you think that the Greeks believed that the sacrifice of animals would please the gods?

Pythagoras   (6 mins)

For this assembly, the teacher will need 27 counters, a sea shell, a record player or piano and a flower

A glance at the map can tell you a great deal about ancient Greece. In the south, there is a ragged coastline, and many clusters of islands offshore. Towards the north there are great mountain peaks, each rising in its own solitary splendour. The geography explains the military situation very well. In ancient times, invading armies from the north had immense difficulties in the high mountain passes and came finally to the dead end of the peninsula. There was no easy route for warring armies in ancient Greece, and most of the time people lived in peace.

Yet living was not altogether easy. The way to travel in ancient times was by boat, and fishing was an important industry. But there were many treacherous seas along the rugged coasts. And living on the land required a man to be agile, a good climber. He must wrest food from the mountain sides, and from the goats he reared. A man need not starve. He could have fish, goat-meat, cheese, wine and olive oil — but to have them he must be resourceful, sharp of eye, clean of limb, not a spare ounce of fat. These are the very qualities to be observed in the statues which were sculpted at the time. It explains why the ancient Greeks loved athletics, why they admired physical beauty, sharpness of mind and independence of spirit.

By the eighth century B.C. this remarkable country, divided by mountains and sea, had created independent pockets of civilization called the city states − Corinth, Sparta, Athens − separate yet sharing a common language. They traded, they grew strong, they colonized. Their ships went everywhere, and there were Greek city states in southern Italy, Sicily, and on the shores of the Black Sea. Their contacts with the outside world brought them knowledge, to be used and then to be developed. The Greek alphabet was acquired from the Phoenecians − the busiest sea-trading people of the ancient world. But the Greek alphabet was longer. The Phoenecian consonant Aleph became the Greek vowel Alpha. The decision to add vowels to the alphabet was an important step forward in the art of writing. But the land in which they lived had also a magical quality − conjuring up stories and legends from the twilight of the imagination. The ancient Greeks were practical people − colonizing, developing trade and the alphabet. But they were also haunted by a heroic, half-remembered history. It was recounted and passed on by story-tellers and poets, and told of legends of gods and goddesses, heroes and heroines, battles with monsters and the entrancements of the song of the sirens. The stories can be found in writings like Homer's Odyssey.

And the Greeks developed skills in mathematics. But in those early times, people had not yet separated learning into different subjects − literature, music, mathematics or art. All learning was called 'philosophy' − the love of wisdom. In the sixth century B.C., there was a Greek philosopher called Pythagoras. He lived, not in Greece but in a city state in southern Italy called Croton. This was one of the Greek colonies.

The teacher produces the counters

Look at this.

The teacher arranges a triangle of three counters while saying the numbers 1+2

The teacher arranges four more counters into a square while saying the numbers 1+3

Numbers taken in order − 1, 2 − make triangles, but odd numbers − 1, 3 − make squares. Let's add to them: 1, 2, 3 . . . 1, 3, 5.

The teacher adds 3 to the triangle and 5 to the square. Then the teacher arranges even numbers into a rectangle while saying 2+2+2
And even numbers come out rectangular. Numbers make patterns.
Pythagoras was intrigued by the patterns. He began to see numbers as governing the whole of existence.

The teacher produces the shell and turns it round to examine the pattern

He saw an inherent proportion in everything, a harmony. The beautiful regular pattern in this shell can be worked out mathematically.

The teacher puts the shell down, and plays a little music

Pythagoras loved music, but he also saw a relationship — a ratio between the notes. What does that word 'rational' mean? It means knowing the 'ratios' — getting things in proportion.

We know very little about Pythagoras. None of his writings have survived. But the patterns he noticed in shells, in music, in triangles led him to study the proportions of things.

The teacher looks into the flower

Have you ever noticed the intricate patterns within a flower? They intrigued Pythagoras. And a further thought struck him. The flowers will die, the musical notes will fade away, but the patterns themselves are always there, repeated in the next flower, the next shell, the next note of music. The patterns are changeless, eternal. Pythagoras saw them as part of a supernatural order of things — abstract, beautiful, part of religion. It led Pythagoras to a mystical kind of religion.

In school, pupils have a habit of moaning because they have to learn his theorem. You remember? The square on the hypotenuse of a right-angled triangle is equal to the sum of the squares on the other two sides. What is it about? It's about the ratios, the proportions, the harmony of a right-angled triangle — typical of the philosopher Pythagoras.

QUESTIONS FOR DEBATE

1. Can you suggest other examples of patterns which reappear time and time again?
2. What advantages do you think there are in separating learning into different subjects such as literature, music, mathematics and art?

Socrates   (6 mins)

The market place in ancient Athens was surrounded by great colonnaded public buildings. They were used for all kinds of purposes — weights and measures, the giving of lectures, public debates and government of the city. Athens was an independent city state. On the great rock of the Acropolis which hung above the market place, were the magnificent temples of the city gods. No city in the ancient world had bolder architecture, finer sculptures or a more elegant appearance. Yet the market was a busy jostling place, full of life:

READER

You will find everything sold together in the same place at Athens: figs, witnesses to summons, bunches of grapes, turnips, pears, givers of evidence, roses, medlars, porridge, lawsuits, chickpeas, myrtle, waterclocks, laws, indictments.

Those are the words of an Athenian playwright. The Greeks would argue about anything — the price of a turnip, or the most abstract of concepts. In such communities as those Greek city states, people of all types were thrown together, a fertile breeding ground of ideas.

The stalls of the Athenian traders were in the open spaces of the market place. There were cobblers, perfume sellers, barbers, money changers, armourers, sausage makers. Imagine, if you like, a cobbler's stall. The cobbler's name was Simon. He and his men made shoes, belts, straps, and reins and saddles for the horsemen. And, while they worked, they talked. In most places it would be no more than homespun discussion at the local shop. But towards the end of the fifth century B.C., the great philosopher Socrates might come along. Simon welcomed him to his stall:

READER

I marvel and applaud, if being but a cobbler, you were wise enough to persuade Socrates and the fairest, best-born youths to sit with you . . .

That quotation is not authentic, but it describes the behaviour of Socrates very well. Socrates was interested in everything, and in everybody — a man who asked questions, so penetrating and with such clarity of thought that he could make people look foolish, especially politicians, which is why he was popular with the young.

People warned their friends about the power of his questioning:

READER

> You do not seem to know that whoever becomes involved in discussion with Socrates, no matter what the topic is, cannot help but be led on by him until he has given a complete account of himself; and Socrates will not let go until he has well and truly sifted him.

Few men in history have permanently affected human thought without writing a single word. I can think of Socrates . . . and of Jesus of Nazareth. It could be argued that we know practically nothing about either of them. In the case of both, we have to trust what other people have said or written about them — especially Plato, the youth who became Socrates' most famous pupil.

Socrates undoubtedly annoyed all kinds of people. He questioned tradesmen like Simon so that it became clear that he understood their work better than they did. But his lively conversation brought extra customers, and they were pleased to see him. It was not so easy, however, for him to keep on good terms with the politicians of his day. At one time in his life, the Thirty Tyrants ruled Athens. Democracy had been overthrown. During this period, Socrates and four other citizens were ordered by the Tyrants to bring in a man called Leon for execution. The other four went to get Leon, but Socrates quietly went home. He did not wish to be involved in an execution ordered by the Tyrants. Later, he commented about the Tyrants:

READER

> I would find it marvellous if a cowherd who reduced the number and value of his flock did not admit being a bad herdsmen, and still more marvellous if the governor of a city who reduced the number and quality of its citizens was not ashamed and did not think himself a bad guardian.

The homely comparison was a very effective criticism. . . and likely to anger the Tyrants. From the descriptions of him, Socrates was a squat, stumpy man with large eyes, thick lips and a considerable belly. At one point, Socrates tried to convince a man called Cristobulus that the way to judge beauty was by seeing how useful the parts of the body are:

READER

> Your eyes see only straight ahead, but mine see also to the side, since they stick out. Your nostrils look to the ground, but mine flare so as to receive smells from all sides. My flat nose does not block my vision but allows my eyes to see whatever they wish.

Socrates was, of course, joking — but it was still difficult to argue with him. All his life, Socrates remained a poor man. His shrewish wife, Xanthippe, was always complaining of his failure as a breadwinner. When they were particularly short of money, she sometimes became very angry indeed with him, much to the amusement of the passers by:

READER

> Once when she tore off his cloak in the market place and his friends urged him to hit back, he said 'Yes indeed, so that while we spar you may egg us on with "Good hit, Socrates! Well done Xanthippe".'

The truth of the matter was that Socrates much preferred spending his time in discussion to anything else — and he saw no particular need of riches. At the age of seventy, after spending his life in and around the market place, Socrates was brought to trial. His questions had angered too many important people. What did they say were his crimes? He was accused of corrupting the young, and of neglecting the city gods. Socrates stuck to his principles as he defended himself:

READER

> I owe greater obedience to God than you, and so long as I draw breath and have my faculties, I shall never stop practising philosophy, and exhorting you, and elucidating the truth for everyone I meet. . .

Socrates, as you might expect, was found guilty. But he could have avoided the death penalty. All he had to do was to agree to leave Athens and to go into exile. But if Socrates was curious about life, he was also curious about death. He chose to accept the death penalty and, when the time came, took the draught of hemlock which ended his life. He talked to his friends right up to the end. His condemnation was one of the tragedies of the ancient world.

QUESTIONS FOR DEBATE

1. Why do you think Socrates was found guilty? Would he fare any better in modern Britain?
2. Do you think that Socrates was right when he said that he owed greater obedience to God than to the magistrates? Is that a dangerous thing to say?

Delphi   (4 mins)

Athena and Poseidon were the two main divinities of ancient Athens, although shrines and altars to many other gods and goddesses were also to be found in the streets and squares of the city. Elegant statues and paintings of a multitude of divine beings could be seen everywhere — not simply on the Acropolis, the main religious centre of the city in the Golden Age.

The religion of the Greek city states was as complex and as varied as the people themselves. Some gods and goddesses were sacred only to a particular place. Such deities had probably developed out of ancestor worship. But as well as the local cults, there was also the religion common to the whole of Greece. It had grown out of their mythology, their legends and their poetry — expressed particularly in the great epic poems of Homer. These gods and goddesses, so it was said, lived in a divine and elaborate society at the top of Mount Olympus. And there was a great national shrine to Greek religion in the hills at Delphi.

The Greeks considered the Temple of Apollo at Delphi to be the centre of the world. The exact spot was marked by a stone called the 'omphalos' — the word means 'the navel'. The contradictory nature of the Greeks and their religion was emphasized at Delphi. The shrine was sacred to Apollo, the god of reason and law. But it was sacred also to Dionysus, the god of wild exuberance and passion. If human beings were a remarkable mixture of reason and passion, then so were the gods. Delphi was dedicated both to order and to disorder, both to reason and to passion, both to law and to exuberance. The setting said it all. The temples at Delphi were serene, orderly and classical, yet they were built in a magical, wild and turbulent countryside.

At the heart of the rites at Delphi was the oracle — a priestess called Pythia who sat on a bronze tripod and went into a trance. She then delivered her message in words quite incomprehensible. No important decision was taken by the Greeks of the ancient world without first going to Delphi to consult the oracle. Socrates consulted her, and so did many other private citizens. And if the city fathers of Athens, Corinth, Sparta or any of the other city states wanted advice, it was to her that they went. It was not possible to understand her words directly, but her sayings were interpreted by one of the priests of the temple of Apollo. There was usually more than one way of understanding the answer. In a sense, people believed what they wanted to believe. Yet the priests at Delphi were also able to influence events.

The world has remembered the genius of classical Greece − in particular the order and proportion shown in the works of the architects and sculptors, the clarity of thought taught by the philosophers. Yet there was much more to it than even those great achievements. Human beings are not always rational. Strong feelings and superstitions play their part. The Greeks allowed scope for such human reactions.

QUESTIONS FOR DEBATE

1. Do you think emotional reactions are as important as logical thought?
2. In the course of time, people rejected Greek religion. Why do you think that happened?

Rhetoric   (4 mins)

'Brand Y is good, but Brand X is brilliant!' Notice, the sentence is divided into two, and the rhythm of the two parts is the same except for the last word.

The teacher beats out the rhythm

It's really much more ingenious than it seems at first sight. Rhythm is part of living − the rhythm of breathing, the rhythm of the heart-beat, the rhythm of walking or running. Without rhythm we would not be alive. And we are all very clever at picking up extra rhythms. That is one of the reasons why people enjoy music. Notice, the repetition of a rhythm is at the heart of all music, no matter what kind you like. In this little sentence a repetition of the rhythm has also been used. 'Brand Y is good, but Brand X is brilliant' − the sentence has used the rhythm so that the word 'brilliant' stands out from all the other words. It makes you notice the brilliance of Brand X.

When the Greeks had their city states in Sicily in the fifth century B.C., a man called Corax and his pupil Tisias were asked to speak in court on behalf of some landowners. The landowners wanted to recover their rights after a period of dictatorship. Corax and Tisias were the first people to think of how language could be used effectively to draw the attention of an audience. It was the beginning of a study of the art of speech-making called rhetoric − the idea that patterns and rhythms in language can be used to persuade people. It is generally believed that Corax was the first person to write a book called *The Art of Rhetoric*, although no copy has survived. Rhetoric, from then on, supplied the rules for speech-making in the ancient world.

But what were the skills to be learnt by the speech-maker? The famous Roman orator, Cicero, was an expert in the art. He successfully argued the cases of his clients before the law-court in ancient Rome. And he made a list of the rules of speech-making. The orator, he said 'must first hit upon what to say'. That is the first step in the preparation of any speech. Then the speech-maker must put his discoveries in order, with a discriminating eye for the importance of each idea in relation to the other ideas. Some ideas must be stressed more than others because they are more important to what the orator is saying. A speech must be in the proper proportions.

Those are the bare bones of the speech, but Cicero goes further. He says that the ideas must then be ornamented with style. Which is the more effective? To say 'Brand X is a good product', or to say 'Brand Y is good, but Brand X is brilliant'? That's what Cicero means when he says that the ideas must be ornamented. Some ways of saying things are far more effective than others. Cicero, and people like him, developed all kinds of tricks of language to catch the attention of the hearer. Some of them are still used − but in poetry rather than in prose. 'My love is like a red, red rose'. . . that's a simile. Similes and metaphors were used as rhetorical devices. Finally, the last task of the orator is to memorize his speech and to deliver it with effect and charm. Reading a speech is nothing like as effective as remembering what you are going to say, and saying it directly to the audience.

The art of persuading an audience was studied with great interest by many people in the ancient world. It was used, in particular, by the lawyers and the politicians. Yet from the very beginning, people had doubts about it. What if a skilled but unscrupulous orator could so sway a crowd that he would convince them to follow an evil course of action? Wars could be started by orators. Innocent men could be found guilty. Murderers could be freed. The great Greek philosopher Socrates called rhetoric 'the art of flattery'. It soon became clear to people that it was important that the orator should be a good man. In the wrong hands, the art of speech-making could lead to disaster.

Various styles of speech-making were developed as time went by. In English, and in most modern languages, the order of words is important. 'The dog bit the man' means something different from 'the man bit the dog'. In Latin, the words could be put in any order. In his speeches, Cicero used to save up the verb to the end of a very long sentence. People would wait with baited breath to hear whether his client had kicked the lady, or had kissed her. Other orators used very short sentences and phrases, piling up the ideas one after the other. You can imagine that such a study of devices in language would lead to more and more complicated rules. By the Middle Ages, when the rules of rhetoric were applied to the making of sermons, somebody commented that it was necessary to be prodigiously learned in order to preach as badly as that.

The rules of the art of speech-making were still considered important in Elizabethan England. If you had been going to school in the age of Elizabeth I, one of the subjects on your timetable would be rhetoric. The Elizabethan schoolboy learnt to make effective speeches in public. It was only with the rise of science in the seventeenth century that people began to object to it. For the description of a scientific experiment, what was required was plain language without ornament of any kind. And people said that irresponsible oratory was one of the reasons for the Civil War between the Roundheads and the Cavaliers. Richard Baxter, one of the great Puritan preachers of the time said, 'I have a strong natural inclination to speak of every subject just as it is, and to call a spade a spade'.

If you were to ask the opinion of most people today, you would probably find that they would agree with Baxter. In the last three hundred years, nobody has even thought of teaching rhetoric in school, or making it once more a serious study. Yet the little devices of language – the ornamentation as Cicero called them – are still with us. Why does the advert say 'Beans means Heinz'? It's rhyme and half-rhyme, with a 'z' at the end of each word. You must admit it's effective. And the twentieth century, too, has suffered from the effects of irresponsible oratory – the speeches of Adolf Hitler.

QUESTIONS FOR DEBATE

1. Everybody has to make a speech at some time in their lives, and people are often nervous on such occasions. Do you think that the art of speechmaking should be taught in schools?
2. What television advertisements have you seen make use of tricks of language?

Jews and Gentiles

Rulers of the Holy Land   (4 mins)

The Israelites moved into the Holy Land from the desert in the thirteenth century B.C. Afterwards, they struggled to possess the land which they believed had been promised by God to their forefather Abraham. Capturing the great Canaanite cities was not easy. But by the reign of King David in the tenth century B.C., Israel had become a major power. David was a brilliant military commander. He subdued all the surrounding nations and created an Israelite empire. Yet his achievement did not last long. At the end of the reign of his son Solomon, the northern tribes turned against the house of David and the kingdom was divided into two. Judah in the south remained loyal to Solomon's son Rehoboam. But Jeroboam, son of Nebat, ruled over the tribes of Israel in the north.

The geographical position of the Holy Land meant that the Israelites were nearly always at war. There were the Egyptians to the southwest, the Assyrians, the Babylonians and the Persians to the northeast. In turn, each of these nations went to war, and always the Holy Land was treated as a corridor for their armies. And when the outside nations were not invading the Holy Land, the Israelites were fighting the local tribes. And when they were not fighting the local tribes, the two Israelite kingdoms were at war with each other. The history of the Old Testament is a history of war.

Between the ninth and the seventh centuries B.C., Assyria was the most powerful nation in the Middle East. The Assyrian empire expanded under a series of powerful rulers. They conducted one military campaign after another through the Holy Land. Assyrian governors were appointed to rule over many of the cities of the northern kingdom. Important Israelites were deported, and foreigners were brought in to take their place. This Assyrian conquest was the end of the northern kingdom. As a result, the tribes who lived in the north became known as the 'lost tribes of Israel'.

In the sixth century B.C., the armies of Babylonia swept through the Holy Land. The city of Jerusalem was captured by King Nebuchadnezzar in 587 B.C. The

Temple, built in the reign of Solomon, was destroyed by the Babylonians. Large numbers of people were taken to Babylonia to work as slaves. About fifty years later, the rise of Persian power put an end to the rule of the Babylonians. The Persians are seen in the Old Testament as the most civilized of all the conquerors of the Holy Land. They allowed the slaves in Babylonia to return to their native country, and they encouraged the rebuilding of Jerusalem and of the Temple. By this time, the only part of the Holy Land which could be described as inhabited by the 'chosen people' was the kingdom of Judah in the south. The religion became known as Judaism, and the people became known as the Jews.

But the story of continuous conquest in the Holy Land continued long after Old Testament times. Next came the Greeks under Alexander the Great. Then, under Pompey in the first century B.C., the Roman legions marched through on their way to Egypt. In the long history of this small country, many rulers have come and gone. The Holy Land had been ruled by Arabic sultans, by Crusaders, by Turks – even by the British. And, even today, the possession of the land is disputed. The conflict between Arab and Jew occasionally erupts into violence.

QUESTIONS FOR DEBATE

1. Can you suggest reasons why the Jewish people have been subjected to persecution from time to time?
2. Do you think the Jews have a right to regard the Holy Land as the 'Promised Land'?

The feast of Purim   (5 mins)

The story of Esther in the Old Testament is set at the time when the Persians had conquered most of the ancient world. They ruled from 539 B.C. until they were defeated by the armies of Alexander the Great nearly two centuries later. The book of Esther is set in the reign of King Xerxes I. He is called Ahazuerus in the Bible. He ruled the Persian empire from his capital at Susa. The luxury and the splendour of life in the royal palace is described in great detail by the biblical writer. Wine is served in golden goblets, and there is much feasting. This is a story set against a background of oriental pleasures.

The story begins when, one day, Xerxes sent a message to Queen Vashti to appear before him. She was to come wearing her royal crown, so that the courtiers could admire her beauty. But the queen refused to come. Her refusal caused such royal anger that Xerxes banished the queen from the court. It took some time before his anger was abated. But eventually Xerxes ordered a search to be made for a new queen. Beautiful young virgins were to be brought before him from all the provinces of the empire. But first they must spend twelve months receiving beauty treatment so that they would be fit for a king. Among these young women was Esther, the adopted daughter of a Jew called Mordecai. Xerxes liked Esther above all the other young women and she became his queen. But Esther did not tell him that she was a Jewess.

The plot thickens when Mordecai heard two of the king's guards planning to assassinate Xerxes. He told Esther about it. She informed the king, and the two men were hanged. About this time, Xerxes promoted a man called Haman to be his chief counsellor. A royal proclamation was made that everyone should bow and do obeisance before Haman. But Mordecai, the Jew, refused to do so. It filled Haman with fury. He not only planned to have Mordecai killed, but also to destroy all the Jews in the empire. He persuaded the king to agree to this and promised that a large sum of money would be paid into the royal treasury when it was done. Letters were sent to all the king's provinces giving instructions that Jewish men, women and children were to be destroyed. And lots were cast, called 'Pur', to decide on which day this should be done.

When Mordecai heard this, he went into mourning. He wore sackcloth and ashes, and went about the city of Susa lamenting loudly. Esther was told about his behaviour and sent him new clothes. But he refused to wear them. Esther then received a message from Mordecai telling her what had been decreed. She must do something about it. But there was a rule in the royal court. Anyone entering the presence of the king unannounced was to be sentenced to death. Only if the king held out his royal sceptre to whoever entered was an exception made. Esther decided that she must take the risk. For three days, all the Jews of Susa fasted as a preparation for Esther's entrance before the king. When she entered, dressed in her royal robes, the king held out his golden sceptre to her, and asked what was her request.

In reply, Esther invited Haman and the king to a feast she had prepared. At the feast, the king again asked what she wanted. In true oriental fashion, Esther did not tell him immediately. Instead, she invited the king and Haman to a second feast the following day. That evening, Haman decided that a gallows should be set up so that Mordecai could be publicly hanged. He would then be able to go to the second feast, enjoying the pleasure of seeing his body hanging there. But that same night, the king could not sleep. He ordered that the record books should be brought to him. There he discovered that Mordecai had passed on the information leading to the conviction of the guards who had plotted to kill the king. 'What honour shall we do to the man who has saved the king's life?' he asked. At that moment, Haman entered the court. He did not know that the king was talking about Mordecai. 'Set a crown on his head and dress him in royal robes,' said Haman in reply. 'Let him ride through the city on the king's charger.' Much to Haman's horror, he was ordered to honour Mordecai in this way.

Later that day, Haman and the king went to the second banquet with Queen Esther. Again, the king asked what was her request. This time, Esther replied. 'I and my people are condemned to death,' she said, 'at the hands of Haman, your chief counsellor.' The story of the book of Esther ends with Haman being hanged on the gallows set up for Mordecai, and with royal permission allowing the Jews in the Persian empire to take revenge on their enemies.

The inclusion of the book of Esther in the Bible is surprising. It is a story of the dangers faced by the Jewish people, and is set against a background of oriental wonders. Esther is celebrated among the Jews every year at the Feast of Purim — so called because, in the story, the lots called 'Pur' were cast to decide when the Jews were to be killed. In Israel, it is a national festival. There are carnivals in the streets, and the story of Esther is read publicly. Whenever the wicked Haman is mentioned in the story, his name is greeted with shouts of derision.

QUESTIONS FOR DEBATE

1. Can the book of Esther be described as a religious book?
2. Why do you think Jewish communities made the Feast of Purim a public holiday?

Hellenism   (5 mins)

The Greek city states were separated from each other by rugged countryside or sea. The best way to travel in ancient times was by boat, and the Greeks had become skilled shipwrights and mariners. Each civic community developed independently of the others, and each had its own characteristics. Yet there were many links between the Greek cities. They shared a common language. And the main gods and goddesses — Apollo, Zeus or Aphrodite — were worshipped everywhere. The Greeks too shared a love of athletics, and an admiration for the human form which expressed itself in their elegant sculptures.

But great civilizations rise and fall. By the end of the fifth century B.C., the decline of the Golden Age of classical Greece was already evident. It was a civilization undermined by a bitter civil war led by Athens on one side and Sparta on the other. And, in the following century, there came Alexander the Great. The Greeks saw him as the barbarian from the north. His armies overcame the power of Persia and swept like wildfire through the eastern world. And with his coming, two things, quite contradictory, happened. The confident society of the Golden Age of classical Greece was no more. The independence of the city states was undermined. Even the gods and goddesses were no longer trusted. Atheism abounded. Yet Alexander took the Greeks with him. He saw himself as the leader of Hellas, the epitomy of the Greek spirit.

Alexander's empire was, in his day, the greatest the world had ever known. It extended from India in the east to Egypt in the west. But it did not last long. In 323 B.C., Alexander was taken ill after a banquet and a drinking bout. He died ten days later. He was only thirty three years old. After Alexander's death, the empire was carved up among his generals.

In the years that followed, trade in the ancient world expanded enormously. Goods from China and India crossed the Afghan passes to be sold in the west. Trading ships plied the coastlines of distant countries. And with the international trade, came a great mixing of populations. Greek cities were built everywhere. Greek was developed as a universal language. That word 'Hellenism' has been coined to describe this culture, coming in the first place from the Greeks, yet infused with ideas from many sources. Temples to the Greek gods were built in many countries. But people also became interested in other religions — particularly the mystery religions of the east. Sorcery, magic, astrology, cults of all kinds were practised in the Hellenistic world.

The spirit of this age was unwelcome in the Holy Land, although many Jews of the time accepted the new lifestyle — especially the rich. In the second century B.C., the high priest at the Temple was called Joshua. But he had changed his name to Jason — a Greek name instead of a Jewish name. Then he went further. He began to think that the God of Israel should be called Zeus. He was strongly supported by Antiochus Epiphanes, ruler of this part of the empire. Shrines to the Greek gods were built in every city and village in the Holy Land. Sacrifices were made to Zeus at the Temple. The practice of the Jewish religion was prohibited. A gymnasium was built in Jerusalem and games were held.

So did the Greek spirit come into mortal combat with the ancient religion of Israel. The identity of the 'chosen people' was under attack. It was bound to lead to revolution. Mattathias was an aged priest living at Modim in the hill country outside Jerusalem. When he was ordered to carry out sacrifices to the Greek gods, he refused. And when another priest was sent to carry out the ritual, he killed him. Mattathias and his sons fled to the hills and took up arms against their Hellenistic masters. The story of their heroic struggle is to be found in the two books of the Maccabees, sometimes included in copies of the Bible.

QUESTIONS FOR DEBATE

1. What similarities can be seen between the Hellenistic world and the world of today?
2. Why do you think Hellenism aroused such strong feelings among the Jews who took their religion seriously?

Jericho   (4 mins)

The agricultural wealth of the oasis at Jericho was prized from the earliest times. The first inhabitants were nomadic hunters who built a sanctuary in about 9,500 B.C. The city itself was inhabited for about eight thousand years — destroyed and rebuilt many times. Then, sometime in the fourteenth century B.C., the mound created from the debris of successive civilizations was abandoned. Perhaps, as it's described in the book of Joshua, the Canaanite city was finally destroyed by the Israelites. But people continued to cultivate the oasis long after. The Old Testament more than once calls Jericho 'the city of palm trees'. Always gardens and orchards abounded.

The fertility of the region and its strategic importance, on the eastern approaches to Jerusalem, meant that the land around Jericho was always cultivated and always defended. In Old Testament times, the mound was at times re-occupied. Later, successive rulers of the Holy Land built many forts in the vicinity. These forts at Jericho were taken by Pompey the Great during the Roman invasion of the Holy Land in 63 B.C.

Octavius, later to become Caesar Augustus, emperor of Rome, presented Jericho to King Herod the Great in 30 B.C. Here Herod built a fortress called Cypros, on a mound south of the Wadi Qilt — a stream which is dried up during the summer months but which flows in the winter. The mound had previously been occupied by a fortress called Thrax. The ancient Roman road, made famous in Jesus' story of the Good Samaritan, runs nearby. Herod also built his winter residence near Cypros. It was a palace of great opulence. There were baths and a gymnasium, a sunken garden and a swimming pool. The palace itself was supplied with water by aqueducts from the Wadi Qilt. The climate around Jericho in the winter is like an English summer — an ideal place for the palace of a king with a taste for the greatest possible luxury.

In the last decade of his reign, Herod greatly increased the size of his winter palace at Jericho. The earlier buildings were incorporated within a massive new scheme involving developments on both sides of the Wadi Qilt. The two parts of the palace were connected by a bridge over the wadi. The north wing contained a large reception hall, two colonnaded courts and a bath house. This was by far the most luxurious palace built by Herod, superseding even his great hanging palaces at Masada.

When Joseph and Mary made their famous journey from Nazareth to attend the census at Bethlehem before the birth of Jesus, they must have passed by this great palace of King Herod the Great. It was usual for Jews coming from Galilee in the north to travel to Jerusalem along the east bank of the river Jordan. It made the journey much longer, but the country of the Samaritans lay between Galilee and Judea. There was enmity between the Jews and the Samaritans at the time, and it was dangerous for Jews to travel through Samaria. We can imagine Joseph and Mary passing the palace with fear in their hearts. King Herod was renowned for his cruelty and had executed many members of his own family.

The fact that King Herod the Great comes into the New Testament stories of Jesus' birth helps us to date the Nativity. He died at this palace at Jericho in 4 B.C. Jesus must have been born before 4 B.C. It makes nonsense of our dating system.

QUESTIONS FOR DEBATE

1. Why do you think later rulers of the Holy Land built forts instead of rebuilding the city on the mound?
2. If Jesus was born before 4 B.C., do you think we should alter our dating system by at least four years?

Jotapata   (4 mins)

'Jotapata is almost entirely perched on a precipice, cut off on three sides by ravines of such extraordinary depth that when people look down into them their sight cannot reach the bottom'. So does Josephus, the Jewish historian, describe Jotapata. It is, by any standards, an exaggeration. The unexcavated site of the city is high in a mountain range above the table-land of Lower Galilee. But it is by no means perched on any precipice. It occupies the centre of a shallow valley.

The site is interesting because Josephus gives an account of the defence of the city against a Roman army. The Romans, under their general Vespasian, had come to the Holy Land to put down a Jewish revolt against the empire. It had all begun in A.D. 66 when a gang of Jewish zealots climbed the great rock of Massada and slaughtered the Roman garrison. Then the Antonia fortress guarding the Temple in Jerusalem was also taken by the Jews. Finally, the zealots threw out a Roman expeditionary force from Syria. The Holy Land was in Jewish hands for the first time for centuries. Inevitably, the Romans came back. Vespasian's first step was to conduct a campaign in Galilee.

At that time, Josephus was commander of the Jewish forces in Galilee. He went under his original name − Joseph ben Matthias. Vespasian played cat and mouse with his forces, and Jotapata was Joseph's final retreat. In his book, *The Jewish War*, he gives a stirring account of the valour of the Jewish forces under his command, and tells of the suicide pact which the leading Jews of Jotapata made when it became clear that the Romans would take the city. They were hidden, so he tells us, in a deep cave beneath Jotapata. According to *The Jewish War*, the suicide pact was carried out, each man killing his neighbour. At last, only Joseph and one other man were left alive. Joseph then convinced his companion that they should surrender to the Romans.

Afterwards, Joseph became a firm friend of Vespasian. In due course, he was allowed to retire as an imperial pensioner to Rome. He assumed the name Josephus Flavius − Flavius being Vespasian's family name. But despite his role as a traitor to the Jewish cause at that time, his work is greatly appreciated. He spent his time in Rome writing a series of histories of the Jewish people. Without his writings, we would know little of the history of the time.

Usually, Josephus' accounts of events seem to be reasonably reliable. But what he says of the siege of Jotapata is certainly an exception. When Josephus himself was involved in the action, he clearly wished to put his own behaviour in the best possible light. Visitors to the site of Jotapata will notice the entrance to a cave in the tel. But it is not very deep. And it is not in the least likely that the Roman army experienced the kind of difficulties with this siege that Josephus describes.

QUESTIONS FOR DEBATE

1. Do you think the Jews were mistaken in taking on the might of imperial Rome?
2. How would you describe the character of Josephus?

Safed   (5 mins)
(The town is sometimes called Zephat.)

In ancient times, this was a tiny village in the north of the Holy Land, near the peak of Mount Canaan which rises to thirty-thousand feet above sea level. The surrounding countryside is a rugged maze of high mountains and small fertile valleys. The name Safed means 'lookout', and the place is first mentioned by the Jewish historian Josephus. At that time he was called Joseph ben Matthias, and was the Jewish commander of Galilee after their revolt against the Roman occupation of the Holy Land. Safed was one of the places Josephus fortified in preparation for the coming of Roman forces intent on retaking the country.

The Roman army, under their general Vespasian, started the campaign to reconquer the Holy Land by attacking Galilee. Joseph's idea was to control the countryside by means of a series of fortified towns and cities which could signal to each other at night. He believed that they could protect the surrounding countryside and, by means of forays, make communications difficult for Vespasian's army. In the event, the Romans had little difficulty, and the fortified settlements were isolated and fell one after another. After his defeat, Joseph changed sides — and his name.

There was no battle at Safed. But perhaps before, and certainly after the Roman destruction of Jerusalem and the Temple in 70 A.D., Safed became a place of refuge for many of the priestly families fleeing from the south. It was much easier for them to avoid the attention of the Romans if they settled in such a remote and unimportant place. That was the point at which the population of Safed began to increase. In the centuries that followed, many Jewish scholars lived there. Even after the rise of Islam and the Arab conquests of the Holy Land, Jewish scholarship continued to flourish at Safed.

In 1102, the Crusader fortress at Safed was built to control the narrow road through the mountains which connected Damascus to the coastal cities of Tyre and Akko. Although the countryside was difficult to traverse, there was a great deal of trade on that road. Safed became a centre of Crusader rule but, in 1188, Muslim forces under Saladin took the fortress and it became part of the Islamic military system. The fortress was re-taken in 1240 by the Crusaders and they expanded the city into one of the largest Christian centres in the Holy Land. There was also a considerable Jewish population, and Safed became a flourishing place of industry and commerce. The remains of the fortress, even today, are very impressive. A moat, forty feet wide and fifty feet deep, has been cut into the rock all the way round, and the fortress was further defended by a double wall seventy feet thick and incorporating seven defensive towers.

Later in the Middle Ages, there were internal struggles within the Jewish religion. Just as Christians disagreed about their faith, so did the Jews. There were two conflicting branches of the religion — those who wished to accept the laws of Judaism as they stood, and those who wished to philosophize about them. At the same time, the Jews were unpopular in many European countries in the Middle Ages. All Jews were expelled from France, for instance, in 1306. They were expelled from Spain in 1492 and from Portugal in 1497 and again in 1506. The effect of these persecutions led the rabbis to wonder why such catastrophes befell their congregations. One particular group of rabbis, convinced that the coming of the Messiah would be heralded by disasters of all kinds, established their community at Safed. Expecting the dawn of a new era, they cultivated mystical contemplation and good works. The doctrines expounded there spread throughout the Jewish world. It led to the establishment of the town as a centre of Jewish mysticism. The Kabbala, as it is called, is still the principal mystical system of Judaism.

The Hebrew printing press established at Safed in 1577 was the first in the Middle East to use movable type. In the eighteenth and nineteenth centuries, there were conflicts between the Jews at Safed and the local Arab communities, and the city suffered a destructive earthquake in 1837. In modern times, the city has attracted colonies of artists inspired by the wild beauty of the surroundings of Upper Galilee. The remains of four Mediaeval synagogues remind the visitor of the beginnings of Jewish mysticism.

QUESTIONS FOR DEBATE

1. Why do you think the towns and cities of the Holy Land have been occupied by so many different foreign powers at various times?
2. What do you think the word 'mysticism' means?

Jesus of Nazareth

Jesus in his time   (6 mins)

Jesus of Nazareth was born in Bethlehem in the Judean hill country towards the end of the reign of King Herod the Great. Herod died in 4 B.C., and it is therefore likely that Jesus' birth was in 6 or 7 B.C. Although he was born in Judea in the south of the Holy Land, the years of Jesus' childhood and early manhood were spent in the north − in a Galilean village called Nazareth. Little is known of the village at the time. It was a remote hillside community overlooking the flat table-land of the valley of Jezreel. There Jesus spent the first thirty years of his life.

The period in which Jesus lived was one of increasing political instability in the Holy Land. Although King Herod had an evil reputation which was entirely justified, his reign had been a period of peace for the Jewish people. He knew how to keep on good terms with the Roman authorities and, while he was disliked by his Jewish subjects, he managed to keep his relationships with them under control. After Herod's death, the kingdom was divided up among three of his sons.

Unlike Herod, the three sons were not pronounced kings. The Romans allowed them instead the title of 'tetrarch'. Jesus was brought up in the territory of Herod Antipas, tetrarch of Galilee. To the northeast was the territory of Philip, tetrarch of the Golan. These two brothers ruled successfully for some years. But in the south the third brother Archelaus, tetrarch of Samaria and Judea, was a failure. When Jesus was about twelve years old, he was removed and his place was taken by a Roman prefect.

The Jews did not like direct Roman rule. In 6 A.D., Quirinius, the Roman governor of Syria, ordered a census of the people. It roused the Jews to fury. They said that counting the population was against their religion. As a result, a revolt against the Romans was started by a man called Judas the Galilean. It made little headway, but it was the beginning of the zealot movement among the Jews, determined to throw off the yoke of Roman power. During the whole of Jesus' lifetime, tension between the Jews and their Roman rulers was gradually building up. It was not to explode into violence until the Jewish revolt more than thirty years after Jesus' death.

At Nazareth, Jesus became the village carpenter. He was the eldest son, and therefore inherited the family business. By the time he was thirty, his father, Joseph, was dead but his mother, Mary, was still alive. The story of his mission began when Jesus suddenly left Nazareth and went to the Jordan valley to be baptized by John the Baptist. John was a phenomenon. The authentic voice of prophecy had not been heard in Israel for centuries. Yet suddenly a prophet had appeared. People went out into the desert to listen to his harsh judgements on the state of the nation. As a sign of change, John baptized his hearers in the Jordan − a ritual washing. Jesus' encounter with John marked the beginning of his ministry. After his baptism, Jesus went into the desert to prepare for his work.

When Jesus went home to Galilee, he did not return to his native Nazareth. Instead, he settled in the thriving lakeside community called Capernaum, on the north shore of the Sea of Galilee. There were many advantages to this. Capernaum was on the road which led from Galilee through the Golan to Damascus. There was a busy market involved in international trade. It was a community drawing much wealth from agriculture and fishing. It was also a centre of taxation, and there was a small Roman garrison. There were opportunities for Jesus to contact the people of many different origins who mingled at Capernaum.

The local synagogue was under the jurisdiction of the Pharisees. At first there was no great conflict between them and Jesus. But later, tensions grew. To avoid controversy, Jesus and the disciples wandered the towns and villages of the Galilean countryside. Jesus attracted large crowds and taught the people by means of parables − stories with a religious meaning which lingered in the mind long after he had told them. He was also famous for his miracles. He cured many people suffering from serious illnesses.

After about three years of ministry in Galilee, Jesus moved south and centred himself on Jerusalem. It did not take long before his teaching infuriated the authorities at the Temple. They requested the Roman prefect that Jesus be executed. Pontius Pilate did not wish to be involved in Jewish squabbles, but during the feast of the Passover, Jerusalem was a flashpoint likely to lead to civic disorder. The sensible reaction from his point of view was to agree to the crucifixion of a troublesome Galilean. But within a very short time, it was reported that Jesus had risen from the dead and that he was, once more, with his followers.

QUESTIONS FOR DEBATE

1. Do you think it surprising that Jesus lived quietly in Nazareth until he was thirty years old?
2. How do you think Jesus' family and the other residents of Nazareth viewed his sudden change in behaviour?

Jesus' parable of the sower   (4 mins)

Many of the stories which Jesus of Nazareth told are well known because they are recorded in the New Testament. You might think that there is nothing more to say about them. The parable of the sower, for instance, is told in the three gospels of St Matthew, St Mark and St Luke and, in each case, the same explanation of the parable is given. Here is the story from St Mark's gospel:

READER

Listen! A sower went out to sow. And as he sowed, some seed fell along the path, and the birds came and devoured it. Other seed fell on rocky ground, where it had not much soil, and immediately it sprang up since it had no depth of soil; and when the sun rose it was scorched, and since it had no root it withered away. Other seed fell among thorns and the thorns grew up and choked it, and it yielded no grain. And other seed fell into good soil and brought forth grain, growing up and increasing and yielding thirtyfold and sixtyfold and a hundredfold.

That's the story as it is told in the gospels. Jesus was very skilful in the way in which he used the ordinary sights and sounds of everyday life as the basis for his stories. But there are a number of points to be made before we can understand what he was saying.

First Jesus lived in the Holy Land — a country with a climate quite different from our own. It is rare for us to have sunshine so hot that it withers shoots of corn. But in Jesus' part of the world, it was quite common. Secondly, Jesus lived nearly two thousand years ago. Methods of agriculture have changed a great deal in two thousand years. Nowadays, we have machines to plough the soil and to sow the seed. We do it in that order — first we plough, then we sow into the open earth. In Jesus' time, the order was different. Farmers ploughed after the seed had been sown. Finally, the story which Jesus told was understood quite differently by the time it was written in the gospels.

Yet it's possible to guess what was said in the first place. 'Look at that farmer,' said Jesus pointing at a nearby field. 'He has all that seed. But what is he doing with it? He's throwing it all over that field — even into the thorns and on the path which people have beaten across his land. Don't you think it's mad to throw valuable seed away?' You can imagine Jesus' audience laughing. The people knew very well that the only way to grow more corn was by sowing the grain onto the land. They also knew that, afterwards, the farmer would hitch up his oxen to a plough and turn over the land. It didn't matter that the seed had fallen in the thorns or on the path. The plough would cut up the path and would tear up the thorns. By the time the farmer had done that, the seed would be safely into the earth and would start to grow. Only in rocky soil would that not be possible.

But what explanation of the parable is given in the gospels? Let's read what St Mark says:

READER

> The sower sows the word. And these are the ones along the path where the word is sown; when they hear, Satan immediately comes and takes away the word which is sown in them. And these in like manner are the ones sown upon rocky ground, who, when they hear the word, immediately receive it with joy; they have no root in themselves but endure for a while; then when tribulation of persecution arises on account of the word, immediately they fall away. And others are the ones sown among thorns; they are those who hear the word, but the cares of the world, and the delight in riches, and the desire for other things, enter in to choke the word, and it proves unfruitful. But those that were sown upon the good soil are the ones who hear the word and accept it and bear fruit, thirtyfold and sixtyfold and a hundredfold.

It's worth remembering that the gospels were written quite a long time after Jesus' lifetime. The situation had changed. In Jesus' time, great crowds of ordinary people were glad to hear his teachings. But by the time St Mark came to write his gospel, there was an organized Church and a growing community of believers. It's possible to see why Jesus told the story in the first place. And it is also possible to see the way in which the writers of the gospels used it.

Jesus compared himself to the sower. Just as the sower threw his seed all over the field, so Jesus delivered his message − the 'word' as it was called − to all kinds of ordinary people. 'That farmer is no fool,' said Jesus. 'He knows that if he scatters the valuable seed on his field, he will receive a great harvest. In the same way, if I scatter the word, God will receive a great harvest of believers.' Jesus' purpose was to give the ordinary people of his time hope. He taught everybody, no matter who they were. But by St Mark's time, the followers of Jesus had formed themselves into a Church. By then, the idea was to get people to persevere. So the explanation of the parable that is given in St Mark's gospel pours scorn on the failures − the people who did not take in what was said to them, the people who had no depth and the people who were distracted by other interests.

In the Christian religion, the harvesting of the fruits of the earth has often been compared to a harvest of believers. It was, in the first place, Jesus' idea. But his followers have used it in many different ways.

QUESTIONS FOR DEBATE

1. Do you think that the writers of the gospels were wrong to use Jesus' stories to their own ends?
2. Do you think it important that people should persevere with their religion?

The Prodigal Son   (6 mins)

'Do you know about the farmer and his two sons?' asked Jesus. 'A couple of years ago, the younger son asked his father if he could receive his inheritance immediately. Farming bored him, and he did not want to wait for the money.' Jesus was sitting on the edge of a water-trough in the square of a small village in the Judean hill country. The heat of the day was over, and it was pleasant sitting there under the olive trees. Around him, squatting on the ground, was a group of serious-looking men. They were Pharisees from the local synagogue. Many of them had already heard the story. It had been common gossip for months. But Jesus was a controversial figure, and these men were quite prepared to hear the story again. Jesus had, so it was said, a way of giving stories new and unexpected meanings.

They listened quietly while Jesus continued. But many of them had reservations about him. He and his disciples had come to the village only that morning, and already there was talk that these men did not take the law of Moses seriously – a grave charge so far as the Pharisees were concerned. It was said that Jesus spent time with sinners – people who did not keep the law. There was even a rumour that he was prepared to sit at table with them and share their meals.

'You know that once that young man had received the money,' said Jesus, 'he immediately went off abroad. For months he had cash to burn. Every night he was out on the town, visiting the gambling casinos, spending his inheritance on wine, women and song.' One or two of Jesus' listeners shook their heads in horror as they imagined it. No good Jew would behave in such a fashion. The law of Moses led to good, clean living.

'Well,' said Jesus, 'you know what happened? There came a time when the money ran out. At first it didn't worry the young man. He thought that he had made many friends who would help him out. But nobody did. Everybody deserted him. And, when he started looking for a job, his luck really ran out. The only work he knew anything about was farming. But there was a great drought, and nobody wanted to hire farm labourers. The only job he could get was as a herdsman to some pigs – the most degrading of all occupations so far as a Jew was concerned. Sometimes he was so hungry that he ate the pig swill in order to keep himself alive.

'It did not take long,' said Jesus, 'before the young man began to think of his father and the home that he had left. "No labourer on my father's farm," he said to himself, "suffers as I do. I will return home, ask my father's forgiveness and see if he will employ me." The young man was still a long way from the house,' said Jesus, 'when his father noticed his arrival. The old man became very excited. Servants were sent out to greet his son. They brought clean clothes and rings to put on his fingers. And a young goat, specially fattened for such an occasion, was killed so that a feast could be prepared. "This, my son," said the old man, "was dead and is alive again; he was lost and is found."

'When the elder brother came from the fields that evening, he was astonished to hear music and dancing coming from the house.' Jesus glanced around at the intent faces of his audience. He could see them imagining the righteous indignation of the elder brother. 'How do you think he felt,' said Jesus, 'when one of the servants told him that his wastrel brother had returned, and that his father had laid on a feast? The elder brother was so angry,' said Jesus, 'that he refused to enter the house. His father was obliged to go out to him. "Please," said the father, "try to understand. You have been with me during all this long time. Everything I have is yours. I know what your brother has done. But I cannot help loving him. He is my son." The elder brother looked at his father and began to understand. He could see that his father could not help loving the runaway son.'

QUESTIONS FOR DEBATE

1. Who was the more remarkable person in the story — the wastrel son or the loving father?
2. In what ways does the story imply relationships between God and human beings?

Panias   (5 mins)

The remains of the ancient city of Panias stand on the river Hermon in the north of the Holy Land. Today, it is on the border between the state of Israel and the Lebanon. The Hermon is one of the feeder rivers of the Jordan. In ancient times, the river began where waters spilled over from a deep pool within a cave at the base of the rocks at Panias. The wide stream appeared out of the cave as if from nowhere. This phenomenon puzzled the ancients and there were many theories as to where the water came from.

The Jewish historian, Josephus, tells us that many people believed that the water came from a lake called Phiale higher up in the mountains. Philip, son of Herod the Great and tetrarch of the Golan in the first century, conducted an experiment which seemed to prove it. Chaff was thrown into the lake. In due course, it obediently appeared in the pool in the cave at Panias. But there is no connection between the lake and the river. Clearly, one of Philip's courtiers had wished to please him. In fact, the water comes from the melting snows of mighty Mount Hermon which rises to the north above Panias. Nowadays, as a result of a series of earthquakes, the river no longer flows out of the cave. Instead, it rises out of the ground below the rocks — a sparkling flow running through meadows fringed with poplars and olives.

In the Hellenistic period, after Alexander the Great's conquest of the Holy Land, the magical emergence of a river running out of a cave stimulated the pagan imagination. The name Panias reflects the world of the Greeks, because they dedicated the city to the nature god Pan. Niches can still be seen cut into the rocks near the source of the river. One bears an inscription to Pan and was obviously meant to contain his statue. The rest of the niches were evidently for his retinue of nymphs. In Jesus' time, there was a new city at Panias. The whole place had been rebuilt by Philip, tetrarch of the Golan, and it was renamed Caesarea Philippi.

It was called Caesarea in honour of Caesar Augustus, emperor of Rome, and Philip's own name was added because there was another city called Caesarea on the coast of the Holy Land.

Caesarea Philippi comes into the story of the New Testament at an important moment in Jesus' ministry. After his baptism by John the Baptist and his period in the desert, Jesus had settled at Capernaum on the northern shore of the Sea of Galilee. At the lakeside and in the surrounding towns and villages, he taught the crowds who came to listen to him. And he performed miracles in God's name. During that time, too, he collected and began to train his twelve disciples. But Jesus knew that the period in Galilee could not go on indefinitely. The time was rapidly approaching when he must go to Jerusalem. Yet he did not immediately set off towards the south. Instead, he and his disciples went north, on a long walk through the Upper Jordan Valley to Caesarea Philippi.

His training of the disciples reached a crisis as they approached Caesarea Philippi. 'Who do men say that I am?' asked Jesus. In this way, he obliged the disciples to face the most crucial of all questions. What was the point of his ministry? In reply, the disciples began to give him various answers. 'Some people say you are John the Baptist come back from the dead,' said one. John had been executed on the orders of Herod Antipas, tetrarch of Galilee, and clearly some of the people who heard Jesus saw similarities in the teaching given by the two men. 'Other people say you are Elijah,' said another disciple. That idea was not unexpected. According to the Old Testament, at the end of his life Elijah had been carried up into heaven. Jewish people were for ever expecting him to return.

Jesus, though, was not interested in public opinion. 'But who do you say that I am?' he asked. It was Peter, one of the closest of Jesus' disciples, who went to the heart of the matter. 'You are the Christ,' he said, 'the Son of the Living God.' An important step towards the development of Christianity had taken place within the context of the pagan shrine at Caesarea Philippi.

QUESTIONS FOR DEBATE

1. Why do you think Jesus took his disciples somewhere quiet whenever he wanted them to face difficult questions?
2. What do you think Peter meant when he called Jesus 'the Christ'?

The Christians

Ancient Corinth stood on the narrow neck of land between mainland Greece and the Peloponnese. It was a brash modern city in the first century, built by the Romans. These days there is a canal to take shipping through from one coast to the other. But when St Paul came to Corinth in A.D. 51, there was no canal and this was a city with two ports, one either side of the isthmus. Sometimes ships were dragged on rollers from one port to the other. The east and the west met at Corinth. Sailors from Egypt, Syria and Turkey mingled with ship crews from Spain and Italy. There were probably bar fights every night among the riff-raff, while the rich merchants struck their bargains in the more respectable tavernas.

There were bazaars and shops, great public buildings and temples at Corinth. You can still see the tall columns of the temple of Apollo, and the remains of a row of lock-up shops in the market place. You could find similar shops in any city in the modern world. You might not think that the Christian missionaries would have thrived in such a commercial atmosphere. Yet St Paul visited Corinth for a weekend — and stayed two years. It shows how well he got on.

All you can see if you visit Corinth today are the remains of the city centre. But Paul lived somewhere in the suburbs, a maze of small streets and houses. Every day he probably worked at one of the ports. He was, by trade, a tent maker. But here, very likely he made sails for the ships. He says that he did not accept money from any of the Corinthians. But the real purpose of Paul's stay in Corinth was to spread the good news of Jesus of Nazareth. Nor was he the only missionary to visit the city. Peter, Jesus' closest disciple, also stayed there. And there was a preacher called Apollos. We know very little about Apollos.

Sometimes these missionaries preached in the market place. Sometimes they held services in the private houses they visited. Those services were very like the Jewish synagogue assemblies on which they were modelled. Psalms were sung. Prayers were said. And there were readings from the Old Testament. The missionaries and their followers also celebrated the Holy Communion. Bread and wine were shared in honour of Jesus. And, like the Passover feast which Jesus had shared with his disciples on the night of his arrest, the Corinthians sometimes also partook of a meal of lamb with bitter herbs and dates. Many of the ordinary people of Corinth took this new religion to heart. Paul says that not many people in his congregation were wealthy or important.

Later, when Paul had moved on to other towns and cities, he continued to think about the Christians at Corinth. And he wrote letters to them, encouraging them and explaining more about the Christian life. Those letters, when they arrived, were read at the services in Corinth, and copies of them were made to give to other churches. But Paul himself had not been one of Jesus' disciples. To tell the story of Jesus' life required someone who had known him well. One of the early historians of the Church tells us that the Gospel according to St Mark was written from the sermons which Peter preached to his congregations.

The New Testament which you have in your Bibles did not exist when Peter, Paul and Apollos were at work in places like ancient Corinth. Yet you can see the pattern of it emerging even then. Those missionaries, in the years after Jesus' lifetime, wrote letters — we call then epistles — and told stories of Jesus' life — we call them gospels.

QUESTIONS FOR DEBATE

1. Why do you think early Christianity flourished in the brash commercial atmosphere of ancient Corinth?
2. How do you think Paul or Mark would have reacted it they had known that we still read their writings in churches today?

The gospel according to St Mark   (6 mins)

The Gospel according to St Matthew is the first to appear in the New Testament. But there is good evidence that St Mark was the first author to write a gospel. In the Book of Acts, we hear that the leading apostle of the early Church was Peter, Jesus' closest disciple. Later in the same book, there is an account of the way in which the Christian message was spread abroad through the missionary journeys of St Paul. But Mark also comes into the story. In about 49 A.D., he set out on a missionary journey with Paul and Barnabas, but only travelled with them part of the way. We are also told in the New Testament that Mark ended up in Rome. He is mentioned in two of Paul's letters from the city.

When the Book of Acts moves on to concentrate on St Paul's journeys, the activities of Peter are no longer recorded. But in his letters, Paul tells us that Peter visited Antioch and that he also went to Corinth. And there is useful information about Peter not included in the New Testament. The First Epistle of Clement, written in about 96 A.D., tells us that Peter eventually ended up in Rome and that he was persecuted by his enemies there. The earliest clue to St Mark's gospel connects the writing of it with Peter. It is recorded by a man called Papias who was a bishop in Asia Minor in about 130 A.D.

READER

> Mark, who had been the interpreter of Peter, wrote down accurately everything that he remembered, without however recording in order what was either said or done by the Lord. For neither did he hear the Lord nor did he follow him, but attended Peter, who adapted his teachings to the needs of his hearers but had no intention of giving a connected account of the Lord's oracles.

We do not have complete copies of Papias' writings, and know his work only through later quotations. But it seems very likely that Mark was with Peter in Rome and wrote the first gospel there.

Rome was the most important city in the world at that time. Nowhere else could offer such opportunities to draw attention to the message of the new faith. Paul came to Rome under arrest. He had been in conflict with the Jews in Jerusalem and had, as a Roman citizen, demanded that his case should be heard before the Roman emperor. While he was under house arrest in Rome, he wrote many letters to the churches he had founded. His story is recorded in detail in the New Testament. But, in contrast, we don't know how Peter and Mark came to Rome.

But what exactly does Papias mean when he says that Mark 'attended' Peter? In the Jewish synagogues, the 'attendant', or 'hazzan' as he was called, did all the practical things required for the running of a religious assembly. Perhaps Mark did the same work when Peter held a Christian service in Rome. There can be little doubt that Peter's Christian services were very similar to synagogue assemblies. And we can be sure that, during the course of his sermons, Peter told many stories about Jesus.

But Papias also suggests that Peter was not interested in the writing of a gospel. He had, so Papias says, 'no intention of giving a connected account of the Lord's oracles'. It seems likely that St Mark's gospel was written from a series of discon-nected sermons during the last few years of Peter's ministry. But if that is true, we have in St Mark's gospel a remarkable record of stories told about Jesus by a man who knew him very well indeed.

QUESTIONS FOR DEBATE

1. A study of St Mark's gospel suggests that events were organized by the author in an order which creates a dramatic effect. Do you think that matters?
2. Why is it reasonable to assume that Peter's early Christian services were like synagogue assemblies?

The epistle to the Hebrews   (5 mins)

Many of the books of the New Testament are either letters, or accounts of the good news of Jesus' words and works, called gospels. But there are also other writings in the New Testament which have, over the centuries, been a source of great puzzlement. The document, called in the Authorized Version 'The Epistle of Paul the Apostle to the Hebrews', is one of those. In our modern translations, St Paul is not mentioned in the title — and with very good reason. The document was not written by Paul. Anybody who can read New Testament Greek would notice at once. 'To the Hebrews' is written in a much better Greek style than anything produced by Paul. And it's not a letter — although somebody has added Chapter 13 at the end to make it look like a letter. The questions about 'To the Hebrews' have tantalized scholars for centuries. We know about the Jews, but who on earth were the Hebrews? And why was the document written? And who wrote it? All we can do is guess. As one early Christian scholar said, 'Whoever wrote Hebrews, God alone knows'.

So let's make an educated guess. Picture a tiny village, say, in the rugged moun-tainous region of Upper Galilee. The people in these houses are Jewish Chris-tians, and they have not lived in this settlement for long. The houses are primitive, built of rough stone — it is really a refugee village. Many of the people have come, perhaps, from Jerusalem where the Christian Church began. But they have moved up here to hide in the barren hillsides because there is war in the Holy Land. The fanatical Jewish nationalists have taken on the might of imperial Rome. It is no place for peace-loving Christian men and women.

The Jewish revolt started in A.D. 66, when a band of zealots climbed the great rock in the desert called Massada and slaughtered the Roman garrison in the fortress on the top. Then the zealots moved on to take the Temple in Jerusalem, and the Antonia fortress which guarded it. From that moment on, violence was in the air. Cestius Gallus, the Roman governor of Syria, moved into the Holy Land with about a third of his forces. But when he got to Jerusalem, it was the beginning of winter. He decided to withdraw to Syria rather than face a long siege. The Jewish zealots dogged his army every inch of the way, attacking by night or in rough terrain. Hardly any of his troops made it back to their Syrian quarters. After that, the Jews ruled the Holy Land for the first time for centuries. But they expected the Romans to come back. They began to make plans and to build fortifications.

The document 'To the Hebrews' was very likely written in a remote Christian village at about that time. It was clearly the work of a Jewish theologian who had been converted to Christianity and who wrote excellent Greek. His purpose was to instruct his followers about the meaning of Jesus' life. And it's obvious from the document that the Roman army had not yet arrived to retake the Holy Land. There are many references to 'the blood of goats and calves' poured out as a result of sacrifices at the Temple. It is enough to prove that the Temple was still in existence and that the sacrifices were still being carried out when it was written. The author of 'To the Hebrews' was very critical of the Jewish sacrificial system.

But what does the author of 'To the Hebrews' tell his followers? It is evident that he wants to link the traditional ideas of the religion of Israel with the words and works of Jesus. He sees Jesus as the Messiah long expected by the Jewish people. But what does that mean? The author turns to one of the psalms in order to explain it. In Psalm 110 there is a reference to 'a priest for ever after the order of Melchizedek, king of Salem'. The ancient Old Testament idea of a very special priestly king in Jerusalem is at the heart of 'To the Hebrews', and the document is a commentary on the psalm. No longer is it necessary, says the author, to sacrifice animals at the Temple. The sin of all mankind is forgiven in the sacrifice which took place on the cross at Calvary.

QUESTIONS FOR DEBATE

1. What reasons can you suggest for the ancient idea that sacrifice is necessary?
2. Why do you think somebody added Chapter 13, making the document look like a letter?

Castellium   (5 mins)

Deep in the Judean wilderness, there stand the remains of a great fortress on the top of a mound. The best way to get there is by helicopter. Anyone approaching at ground level will find that it is necessary to cross a modern artillery range on the way. The fortress was built by King Herod the Great, ruler of the Holy Land in the first century B.C. He was a vassal king of the Roman Empire, and ruled by permission of the Emperor. He is remembered as the wicked King Herod mentioned in the New Testament in connexion with the birth of Jesus of Nazareth. Herod built several such fortresses.

Herod the Great ruled the Holy Land for over thirty years, using his army of mercenaries to keep the country under control. It explains why he built his fortresses. Within the thick walls, deep in the desert, high on a mound and surrounded by his army, Herod was safe from any uprising against his rule. He was a king terrified of his own subjects. The most famous of Herod's desert fortresses is Masada, not far from the shores of the Dead Sea. It was excavated in 1971, and today it is visited by many tourists. But this particular fortress is unexcavated. In Herod's day it was called Hyrcania, and of all his strongholds this was the one with the most sinister reputation. Prisoners taken to Hyrcania were never seen again. Today, the remains of the massive Herodian masonry lie untouched in the desert. The place has remained much the same for centuries.

About seventy years after King Herod's time, there was a Jewish revolt against Roman power. The Jews hated their Roman rulers and, for many years, small bands of Jewish zealots had waged a guerilla campaign against the occupying forces. Open revolt began in A.D. 66, when the zealots took Masada and slaughtered the Roman garrison. At first the Jews were very successful. They destroyed a Roman army which was sent from Syria in the north to put down the rebellion. But eventually the Romans came back with a powerful army and systematically went about destroying the Jewish forces. Jerusalem was re-taken in A.D. 70, and the Temple was destroyed never to be rebuilt. As the Romans took one city after another, the zealots took refuge in the fortresses built in the previous century by King Herod the Great.

The most famous story of this period concerns the re-taking of Masada by the Romans. It involved building a ramp nearly six hundred feet high, and winching a tower and battering ram to the top to smash the walls of Herod's fortifications. The remains of the square Roman camps and the walls which they built around the fortress to stop the zealots escaping can still be seen lying in the desert. But you will find nothing in the history books about the Roman siege of Hyrcania. Yet the square camps and the walls they built there can also be seen lying in the desert around the remains of the fortress. Hyrcania is surrounded by the evidences of war – modern warfare in the case of the artillery range, and an ancient war in the case of the Roman camps and walls.

After the Romans had taken Hyrcania from the zealots, the place was deserted for centuries. Apart from the winter months when it rains in the desert, the terrain is permanently dry. Buildings which decay quickly in our country because of the rainfall are preserved in the desert. The Judean wilderness is one of the world's dry stores. In A.D. 492, a monk called Sabas came to what remained of the fortress. Each year it was his custom to spend Lent in a solitary place. He was the leader of a group of monks who spent their lives in prayer, living in small cells in the Valley of the Kidron a few miles to the north. When Sabas came to this collection of isolated ruins, the desert shepherds called the place Castellium.

The evil reputation of Herod's fortress still remained when Sabas came. The shepherds kept away from it, believing it to be haunted by demons. According to the ancient sources, Sabas sprinkled the remains of the fortress with holy oil, and stayed there in the face of demonic terrors. At last, after supreme effort against his prayers, it is said that the demons left 'with a tremendous din like a multitude of crows'. After Easter of that year, Sabas brought some of his fellow monks to Castellium, and they established a monastery there. The remains of a little church still lie in the desert sand on the top of the mound, surrounded by the fortifications built by King Herod the Great. The visitor can still see the fine mosaic floor of the church in which the monks of the monastery worshipped.

Even today, Castellium is a strange and haunting place. There are the remains of an underground kitchen which has not been used for well over a thousand years. Yet soot still hangs on the rock face above the plaster cooking range, and there is a vaulted brick oven which was used for making bread. There are also the remains of a cistern, to be filled with water when it rained in the desert during the winter months so that it could supply the needs of the inhabitants during the rest of the year. And, most fascinating of all, there are the remains of a mausoleum. The chamber in which the bodies of the monks were buried has collapsed, and one can see a large number of human bones lying there. And, around the remains of the chamber, there are fine wall paintings of saints. What was a place with an evil reputation became a holy place. It is all there for you to see — if you are in the Holy Land and have a helicopter.

QUESTIONS FOR DEBATE

1. Do you think that some places really acquire an evil atmosphere — or is it all in the mind?
2. Why do you think monks like Sabas wanted to spend time by themselves in the desert?

Egeria visits Mount Sinai   (5 mins)

In about the year 381 A.D., a nun called Egeria began a journey which was to take three years. She went on a pilgrimage to the countries where events described in the Bible took place. And she kept a diary so that her sisters at the convent could have some knowledge of her adventures. Much of what she wrote has long been lost, but about a hundred years ago a handwritten copy of the middle of her diary was found in a library in Italy. Probably at the beginning of her manuscript, she gave some idea of where she came from. But now, we can only guess. It seems likely that she was a native of Spain or France, because one of the bishops she met on her travels says that she came 'right from the other end of the earth'.

   The manuscript, as we have it, begins as Egeria is travelling through the rugged desert country of the Sinai peninsula. She says that holy men are with her, acting as her guides. According to the Old Testament, the Israelites had wandered the Sinai desert for forty years after their escape from Egypt. The sight of this countryside brought the story alive so far as Egeria was concerned:

READER

   In the meanwhile, we were walking along between the mountains, and came to a spot where they opened out to form an endless valley — a huge plain and very beautiful — across which we could see Sinai, the holy Mount of God.

There are many great mountains in the Sinai peninsula, but Egeria was told that she had come to the very mountain from which God had given Moses the Ten Commandments:

READER

> It looks like a single mountain as you are going round it, but when you actually go into it there are really several peaks, all of them known as 'the Mount of God', and the principal one, the summit on which the Bible tells us that 'God's glory came down', is in the middle of them. I never thought I had seen mountains as high as those which stood around it, but the one in the middle where God's glory came down was the highest of all, so much so that, when we were on top, all the other peaks we had seen looked like little hillocks far below us.

Egeria was certainly an enthusiastic traveller, and possessed of a lively curiosity. If the mountains of Sinai were there to be climbed, she was going to climb them:

READER

> You do not go round and round them, spiralling up gently, but straight at each one as if you were going up a wall, and then straight down to the foot, till you reach the central mountain, Sinai itself.

You can imagine her struggling up the barren rocks of the mountain range. But the climbing of Mount Sinai was much more than a matter of sightseeing so far as Egeria was concerned. She also took a great deal of interest in the people she met:

READER

> So at ten o'clock we arrived on the summit of Sinai, the Mount of God where the Law was given, and the place where God's glory came down on the day when the mountain was smoking. The church which is there now is not impressive for its size (there's too little room on the summit), but it has a grace all its own. And when with God's grace we had climbed right to the top and reached the door of this church, there was a presbyter, the one who is appointed to the church, coming to meet us from his cell. He was a healthy old man, a monk from his boyhood and an 'ascetic' as they call it here — in fact just the man for the place. Several other presbyters met us too, and all the monks who lived near

the mountain, or at least all who were not prevented from coming by their age or their health.

In Egeria's time, many holy men lived in cells in the deserts of Egypt and of the Holy Land. They usually came together in a church for their services, but they spent the rest of their time in solitary prayer. The arrival of pilgrims like Egeria was clearly an opportunity for quite a large gathering of these men.

While Egeria's description of the visit to Mount Sinai gives us a picture of the mountain itself and the people surrounding it, the main purpose of her visit was religious:

READER

> All there is on the actual summit of the mountain is the church and the cave of holy Moses. No one lives there. So when the whole passage had been read to us from the book of Moses (on the very spot!) we made the Offering in the usual way and received Communion. As we were coming out of church the presbyters of the place gave us 'blessings', some fruits which grow on the mountain itself.

There were two parts to the service Egeria attended in the little church at the top of Mount Sinai. In the first part there were the readings, and in the second part, which Egeria calls 'the Offering', the priest carried out the actions which Jesus performed at the Last Supper.

And what reading did Egeria hear 'on the very spot'? It's quite clear from what she says, and it's worth reading for ourselves:

READER

> And on the morning of the third day, there were thunders and lightnings, and a thick, black cloud upon the mountain, and a very loud trumpet blast, so that all the people who were in the camp trembled. Then Moses brought the people out of the camp to meet God; and they took their stand at the foot of the mountain. And Mount Sinai was wrapped in smoke, because the Lord descended upon it in fire, and the smoke of it went up like the smoke of a kiln, and the whole mountain quaked greatly. And as the sound of the trumpet grew louder and louder, Moses spoke, and God answered him in thunder. And the Lord came down upon Mount Sinai, to the top of the mountain; and the Lord called Moses to the top of the mountain, and Moses went up.

QUESTIONS FOR DEBATE

1. Do you think Egeria was really an enthusiastic tourist who used religion as an excuse for her travels?
2. Can you think of reasons why the Christians built churches on holy sites?

Cana in Galilee   (6 mins)

'On the third day there was a marriage at Cana in Galilee, and the mother of Jesus was there; Jesus also was invited to the marriage with his disciples.' So begins one of the most famous of the New Testament stories about Jesus of Nazareth. According to St John's Gospel, the wine ran out very soon after the wedding feast had begun. We are not told why this happened, and it seems very strange.

The fertile countryside of Galilee is rich in crops of all kinds. Practically anything will grow there, and there are many vineyards. In Jesus' time, it is very likely that the Galileans behaved very much like country people everywhere. Apart from the Sabbath, they worked very hard on the land day in, day out. A wedding was a special occasion – an excuse for a grand village party. The chances are that the feasting went on for days, and that a great deal of wine was drunk. You could not imagine any young couple thinking about getting married unless there was a plentiful supply of wine.

Wine was stored in wineskins in Galilee in the first century. When a goat had been killed for food, the skin of the animal was tanned in water containing the bark of oak trees. The tannic acid in the bark made the skin soft and flexible. But old wineskins eventually became brittle and were liable to burst. In one of Jesus' stories, he warned people not to put new wine into old wineskins. Perhaps the best explanation for the fact that the people catering for the marriage at Cana ran out of wine was that the wineskins had burst.

The New Testament then goes on to tell us how Jesus miraculously turned the water in six large waterpots into wine. It saved the situation. A wedding without wine would have spoilt the occasion for the young couple and their guests. According to St John's Gospel this is the first miracle that Jesus performed. But where was the little village of Cana where all this took place?

A few centuries after Jesus' time, it became the done thing for people to make tours of the Holy Land, visiting the places where Jesus had taught and had performed his miracles. One of the earliest accounts of such a tour was written by a man who called himself the Pilgrim of Bordeaux. He visited the Holy Land in 333 A.D., almost exactly three hundred years after the crucifixion. He does not tell us his name in his writings.

He left his native Bordeaux in southwestern France, and travelled in stages across Europe. He took a boat from Italy across the Aegean to Greece, then crossed into what is now Turkey. Eventually he reached the Holy Land. It must have taken him months on the hot, dusty roads and it certainly cost him a great deal of money. There were good roads in the Roman Empire of his time, maintained by the Roman army. He probably had to pay a toll for each stretch of road on which he travelled, and very likely he hired another donkey at each staging post. Most of the time, the Pilgrim tells us very little about his journey except to give a list of the places at which he stayed. Only when he gets to important places like Jerusalem does he give us more details.

The Pilgrim of Bordeaux was one of the earliest tourists. But many came after him. A nun called Egeria made the journey a few years later. She was probably Spanish, and she wrote an account of what she had seen at the holy places. But the most famous of all those early pilgrims to the Holy Land was St Jerome. After he had wandered around the country with a large company of friends, he started a monastery at Bethlehem and most of his work as a translator of the Bible took place there. The Bible was originally written in two languages. The Old Testament was written in Hebrew. And the New Testament was written in Greek. But in Jerome's time, the people of France, Italy, Spain and North Africa spoke Latin, the language of the Roman Empire. Jerome's translation from the Hebrew and the Greek into Latin was called the Vulgate, the 'book of the people'. It was the most important version of the Bible in western Europe for more than a thousand years after this time.

But what has all this to do with Cana in Galilee? If you travel north of Nazareth, where Jesus was brought up, and follow the road in the direction of Tiberias on the shores of the Sea of Galilee, you will pass through a settlement called Kafr Kana. There you will find a small church, and you will be told that this is Cana, the place where Jesus performed his first miracle. But if you travel northwest of Nazareth, you will find yourself in the flat table land of the Bet Netofa Valley. It stretches for miles. The land is a patchwork of crops of all kinds – cotton, maize, wheat, tobacco, vines. Because the valley is often flooded in the winter months, no main roads pass through this way – only rough tracks. You will see the tents of the Bedouin here and there, looking as they have looked since time immemorial – except that a television aerial is fixed to one of the tent poles.

Take a Landrover – it's the only way. Eventually, you will come to the foothills of the Bet Netofa Range. And tucked into the base of a small valley, you will find Tel Cana – the real Cana of Galilee. There is nothing to see. All that remains of the village is a small mound. No archaeologist has been near it. Perhaps, some day, the experts will start digging and we will see the remains of pottery, of cooking utensils, of a synagogue and of houses from the time of Jesus of Nazareth.

But why is everybody told that Kafr Kana, on the main road north of Nazareth, is on the site where the village of Cana stood in Jesus' day? The misconception has gone on for centuries. When Jerome visited what he thought was Cana in the fourth century, it was to Kafr Kana that he went. But why? If you go to the Holy Land, you will find that there are plenty of guides willing to show you round. It was the same in Jerome's time. And the guides, as long ago as the fourth century, wanted their tours to be convenient . . . on the main roads. To go to Tel Cana was a difficult journey at the best of times, and virtually impossible in the winter months when the Bet Netofa Valley was flooded. But if you go to the real Cana it brings into the mind's eye that little group of people nearly two thousand years ago — Mary, Jesus and half a dozen disciples — making their way across the flat table land on their way to a wedding.

QUESTIONS FOR DEBATE

1. Do you find it difficult to believe that Jesus turned water into wine?
2. Do you think that modern tourists should be told that Kafr Kana is not Cana in Galilee?

Islam

Muhammad the prophet   (5 mins)

Muhammad was born at Mecca in Arabia in about 570 A.D. Because his father had died, he was brought up under the care of his grandfather. When he was six years old, his mother died and, when he was eight, his grandfather also died. Under Arabian custom at the time, children could not inherit property. Consequently, during Muhammad's childhood he experienced poverty. The family belonged to the famous Hashem clan in Mecca, and after the loss of his close relatives, the young Muhammad came under the care of his uncle, Abu Talib. He was the head of the Hashem clan, and took Muhammad with him on some of his trading excursions to Syria.

Mecca was a great centre of trade in this period. Merchants and their pack camels plied from such places as Damascus in the north to the Yemen in the south. They traded in goods which had travelled from as far away as India in the east or Africa in the west. Mecca was a prosperous place, except that the money was in the hands of a small number of merchants. At about the age of twenty-five, Muhammad married a rich woman called Khadijah. She was forty years old but, despite the difference in age, the marriage was a happy one. His wife's money allowed him to set up in trade.

Religious life at Mecca was centred on the pagan shrine called the Kaaba at which there were many idols. Many of the traditional virtues of Arab life were connected with this shrine. But they were in danger of being forgotten in Muhammad's time. The rich merchants pursued their own interests and were less likely than in the past to care for the poor and the unfortunate. When he was about forty years old, Muhammad received a vision which quite astonished him. A heavenly being visited him, and he heard a voice saying, 'You are the messenger of God'. From then on, Muhammad frequently received such visions. He believed that they came directly from God, and that it was his task to pass such knowledge to the rest of mankind. Some of the revelations were treasured in the memories of Muhammad's followers. Others were written down. In about 650 A.D., after his lifetime, they were collected and written in the Qu'ran — the sacred scriptures of Islam. Muhammad gathered many followers who joined him in prayer. To acknowledge the divine majesty of God, they prostrated themselves and touched the ground with their foreheads. In about 613 A.D., Muhammad began a public preaching ministry at Mecca.

Muhammad's preaching, though, was not entirely welcomed. There were reasons for this. Some of the rich merchants at Mecca felt that his religious ideas might harm their trade. Others believed that the Kaaba, the traditional shrine at Mecca, might lose its influence. But perhaps the most powerful reason for the rejection of his teachings was that people suspected that Muhammad would, sooner or later, command political power. The wisdom which he showed was likely to be much respected by the ordinary Arab people. Certainly, pilgrims to the Kaaba from Medina, a settlement around an oasis in the north, showed more respect for Muhammad's teachings than was to be found among the inhabitants of his native Mecca. In 622 A.D., many of the followers of Muhammad migrated to Medina. Muhammad himself was among the last to move.

In the years that followed, Muhammad fought many battles against the people who opposed him. There were three Jewish clans at Medina. At first, Muhammad taught his followers to face Jerusalem when they prayed, and to observe the Jewish festivals. But the Jews regarded him as a false prophet. Muhammad was obliged to change his mind. He told his followers to face Mecca when they prayed, and he expelled the Jewish tribes from Medina one by one. He showed particular ruthlessness when it came to the last of the Jewish tribes. The men were all savagely executed, and the women and children were sold into slavery.

Muhammad also found himself in a struggle against the leading men of Mecca. He raided their caravans and took their goods to build up his treasury. Gradually, he gained the upper hand. In 628 A.D., he made a truce with Mecca, and gained the right for his followers to make pilgrimages to the Kaaba. The truce did not last long. In 630 A.D., some of Muhammad's followers were attacked by a desert tribe allied to Mecca. Muhammad used the occasion as an excuse to attack the city. Mecca capitulated very quickly. The idols were removed from the Kaaba, and the shrine became the centre of the Muslim faith.

Muhammad's teachings have influenced countless generations since his time. He taught his followers to surrender to the will of Allah. He saw himself as nothing more than a messenger — a prophet. He said that God had sent other messengers to different nations. He firmly believed, for instance, in the prophets and teachers of the Old Testament. Muhammad died in 632 A.D. The religious ideas which he had taught had taken firm root.

QUESTIONS FOR DEBATE

1. Could Muhammad and his followers accept the New Testament teaching that Jesus of Nazareth was the 'Son of God'?
2. Women outnumbered men in Muhammad's time. Do you think this led to his allowing polygamy among his followers?

Islamic Jericho   (4 mins)

Muhammad, the founding prophet of Islam, had extended his influence in Arabia both by teaching and by the use of armed force. In the years that followed, the Islamic faith was spread in many ways. Merchants, travelling the trade routes of the Middle East and beyond, took their religious beliefs with them. And the caliphs who inherited Muhammad's political power also continued the process of conquest. In the wake of the spread of Muslim power, a great culture developed. The remains of the Islamic palace at Jericho give the visitor some insight into the way of life developed by the caliphs. The palace illustrates an Arabic culture which made its presence felt in many parts of the eastern world.

The remains of Hisham's Palace at Jericho lie about a mile and a half to the north of Tel es-Sultan — the site of the prehistoric city. The palace was built at the beginning of his reign by Hisham, the tenth Umayyad caliph who ruled between 724 and 743 A.D. In his time the empire was extensive, stretching from Spain in the west to India in the east. This palace is a typical example of the period — a royal complex of luxury and splendour set in a centre of great agricultural wealth. In such a location, the inhabitants could be sure of superb weather and ample supplies of excellent food. Similar private palaces were built by the Umayyads in Syria and in Jordan, although Hisham's Palace at Jericho was the finest of them.

There is a great deal for the modern visitor to see, although the buildings suffered from an earthquake as early as 746 A.D. The remains were covered in sand until, over a thousand years later, they were excavated by English archaeologists in 1937. The Jordan valley is, however, dry for the most of the year, and it has provided excellent conditions for the preservation of such a palace. Early treasures of Islamic architecture and art have survived here.

The palace is approached through a forecourt which contains a square cistern, at one time covered with a dome. While Hisham's Palace is outside the area of the natural oasis at Jericho, it is clear that aqueducts and irrigation schemes were in use. Clearly, in Hisham's time, the palace was surrounded by gardens and orchards, and there was a plentiful water supply in the buildings and courtyards. A gatehouse leads from the forecourt into the palace itself. The main buildings consist of living quarters and halls on two floors surrounding a large rectangular courtyard. Within the palace there is also a small mosque and a subterranean bath house. Wandering around this courtyard, one can imagine the caliph and his followers living in luxury within elegant surroundings.

But it is to the north of the palace itself that the full impact of Hisham's Palace is brought to life. Here are the remains of a very large bath house, no doubt used by Hisham himself together with his favourite courtiers. The walls on the outside of the building are punctuated with niches in which stand male and female figures. And inside this bath house, in a small apse, is one of the finest surviving treasures of early Islamic art. A perfectly preserved mosaic depicts an orange tree beneath which are two gazelles, one being attacked by a lion. The warm colours and fine craftsmanship of this mosaic give a glimpse of the richness with which this palace was once ornamented. This bath house was clearly a hall of pleasure, where men and women not only only bathed but watched entertainments or sang and danced. Perhaps the building was also used for royal receptions. Alongside this bath house, there are also the remains of a fine large palace mosque. Hisham's Palace at Jericho illustrates the great skills in architecture and art developed under the caliphs.

QUESTIONS FOR DEBATE

1. Do you think belief in Islam could be spread by warring armies?
2. Can you think of reasons why such skill and artistry was used for the building of a bath house?

The Bedouin of Sinai   (4 mins)

Few people on earth are as fiercely independent as the Bedouin. They wander the hot waterless deserts with their camels and their flocks of sheep and goats, living as they have lived for centuries. In many ways, they are a vivid reflection of the early stories of the Old Testament when Moses led the Israelites for forty years in the rugged desert country of the Sinai. Although the Bedouin belong to the Muslim faith, they take great pride in the fact that Moses and the Israelites lived much as they do, and coped with the hardships of desert life. Muhammad taught that the prophets and lawgivers of the Old Testament were messengers from God. Moses is a great religious leader in the minds of the Bedouin as well as in the eyes of Christians and Jews.

Like the Israelites of old, the Bedouin tribes live in tents which give them the freedom to move from place to place. As the sparse grasses and the meagre water holes in one location in the desert are exhausted, the tribe moves on to another. A tent can be packed relatively easily, and loaded onto the back of a camel. These tents are woven from the hairs of black goats. During the short winter months it often rains very heavily in the desert. The goat hairs expand when they are wet and make a waterproof cover for the Bedouin family. In the hot summer, the tents are often covered in straw thatching which protects the interior from the penetrating rays of the sun.

The whole of the Sinai desert is divided up so that each Bedouin tribe has its own territory. In each area, there are certain limited sources of water and the tribe has the right to cultivate the land wherever possible. Bedouin eat a great deal of unleavened bread — exactly the food eaten by the Israelites of old at the time of their escape from Egypt. Most of this bread is made from flour bought with money from the sale of animals from their flocks. But it is sometimes possible to grow a patch of wheat in the desert during the rainy winter months. Each year, a camel is hitched to a primitive plough, and the land is prepared. But only once in every four or five years does the crop come to the point at which it can be harvested. In most years, the hot sun dries up the shoots long before the ears of grain have grown.

The Bedouin family is run as a business. A visitor might be surprised to see the men of the tribe sitting around talking and drinking coffee, while the women are hard at work tending the flocks or seeing to the children. Yet the order of things is logical enough in the Bedouin mind. The business in which they are engaged is the raising of flocks. The man of the family is the manager of the business. He buys and sells animals, and finds pasture for the flocks. He maintains contact with the chief of the tribe, and is prepared at all times to fight for the honour and well-being of his dependants. With all these responsibilities, he cannot also be expected to do the ordinary menial tasks which can so easily be done by the women. The women are the labour force of the family business.

Although the Bedouin are members of the Muslim faith, many of their ideas are very unorthodox. They believe in Allah, the one God, and in the teachings of Muhammad, his prophet. They are devout, God-fearing people and their prayers come from the heart. But from time to time, they make visits to the shrines and tombs of holy men. Often such a visit involves the sacrifice of a goat together with prayers for the well-being of the Bedouin family and livestock. Exposed to the dangers of desert life, the Bedouin seek the protection of Allah against many dangers:

READER

> O Allah protect me from the tailed scorpion and the moustachoed millipede, the sidewinding viper and slithering black cobra, and the spider, 'mother of graves'.

The Bedouin, too, have many superstitions. They believe that strangers can cast an 'evil eye' on their families and they shield their children against the glances of passers-by. Sometimes they object to people taking photographs for the same reason.

QUESTIONS FOR DEBATE

1. Do you think life in the desert helps to make people more interested in religion?
2. Nowadays, schools are being set up in the desert for the Bedouin children. How do you think their way of life will be affected?

The Crusades

Nebi Samwil   (5 mins)

The land rises gradually to the north of the Old City of Jerusalem. In the long history of the Holy City, enemies have always approached from this higher ground. The Old City itself stands on two high ridges, and is protected on all other sides by precipitous slopes. Since the earliest times, the northern walls have been better fortified than elsewhere — and with good reason. Any attack on Jerusalem was bound to come from the north.

It is possible to stand on this high ground and view the Old City. The best view-point is Nebi Samwil. A mosque stands high on a spur where it is believed the prophet Samuel is buried. It explains the name 'Nebi Samwil'. The prophet's tomb is within the mosque. And if you climb the long flight of steps up to the minaret, the Old City of Jerusalem, a few miles away, is spread below you. You can see the golden Dome of the Rock, the silver dome of the El Aqsa mosque, the northern walls and the Damascus Gate built by Suleiman the Magnificent. Within the walls, the streets are straight and narrow — the work of the Roman town planners nearly two thousand years ago. But the buildings are in a myriad of styles and shapes, telling the story of the many foreign powers which have occupied this city. The other important thing to do at Nebi Samwil is to examine the mosque itself. It was not always a mosque, but a church built by the Crusaders.

One of the most remarkable scenes in history took place at Nebi Samwil on July 8th, 1099. A Crusader army had arrived there the previous day. There were about twelve thousand foot soldiers and over a thousand cavalrymen — a small fraction of the number of people who had set out from the towns and cities of Europe, wearing the cross and determined to free the Holy Land from the forces of Islam. Their progress across Europe and through Anatolia had been chaotic in the extreme. Their leaders, mostly French, had fallen out time and time again. The forces of Hugh of Vermandois, brother of the King of France, had been much reduced by shipwreck in the Adriatic. Many had died at the long siege of Antioch, and others had been struck down by a plague after the city had been taken.

It had all started with a speech by Pope Urban II in 1095 to a large crowd at Clermont in southern France. Nobody knows exactly what he said, but stories of the sufferings of Christian pilgrims who had visited the Holy Land were rife. And there were many warring factions in Europe. It is likely that the Pope encouraged people to direct their energies to a holy cause. The great popular reaction to his words was astonishing. While the princes were organizing armies, many people became impatient and simply set off. The People's Crusade, led by Peter the Hermit and Walter the Penniless, caused a great deal of trouble in the countries through which it passed. Unable to control his followers, Peter returned to Constantinople to ask for help. While he was away, these Crusaders were ambushed and practically annihilated by the Turks. The Pope had stressed that nobody should set out on this pilgrimage without the highest of motives, but atrocities of all kinds were committed.

But now at last the long journey was over. The Crusaders who had survived were in sight of the Holy City itself. Many believed that Christ would return in power and great glory once Jerusalem was in their hands. The promise of the New Testament would be fulfilled. But the Muslim governor of the city was confident that he could beat off the Crusaders. Jerusalem was in the territory of the Fatimid caliphs of Cairo, Shi'te Muslims. They had captured the city the previous year. The Crusaders were short of supplies, awaiting ships which would bring provisions to the port at Jaffa. The defenders, on the other hand, were well provided with all that they needed to withstand a siege.

But on 8th July, 1099 the Crusaders did not begin the siege. A strict fast was called, and the clergy who were with them led a great procession of princes, knights, infantry and cavalry from Nebi Samwil down in the direction of the Old City. Round the walls they went, while the defenders jeered at them. It was reminiscent of the Israelites of old who marched round and round the city of Jericho. According to the Old Testament, the walls of Jericho collapsed. But that did not happen when the Crusaders came to Jerusalem. So they ascended the Mount of Olives, and heard a fiery sermon preached by Peter the Hermit. The following day, the siege began. After the Crusaders had broken in, there was a great massacre of the inhabitants, both Muslim and Jew. The holy cause had produced yet another unholy scene of death.

QUESTIONS FOR DEBATE

1. Why did the People's Crusade cause such trouble in the countries through which it passed?
2. Was the Pope right to encourage the Crusade in the first place?

Acre   (5 mins)

Accho was the original name of the city. The caravan route from Damascus and the east arrived at the Mediterranean coast here and, from very early times, merchants moved to and fro along that road, buying in one market and selling in another. This was a Phoenecian city, built near one of the few natural harbours in the Holy Land and inhabited by the busiest sea-trading people of the Ancient World. Over the centuries, many foreign powers controlled Accho.

After the death of Alexander the Great in 323 B.C., his empire was carved up among his generals. Accho came into the hands of Ptolemy who ruled Egypt. He changed the name of the city to Ptolemais, and so it remained for the next few centuries. The New Testament tells us that, in 53 A.D. towards the end of his third missionary journey, St Paul spent a day with a colony of Christians at Ptolemais. Later, under the Emperor Nero, the city received the honour of becoming a Roman colony. It was designated 'Colonia Claudia Ptolomais'. In the centuries that followed, Ptolemais flourished and new shipyards were constructed at the port.

The city surrendered to the Muslims in 636 A.D., and called it Akko. This was a period of spectacular Arab conquests leading to the building up of a great Islamic empire. The Umayyad caliphs used Akko as the supply port for their headquarters at Damascus, and the first caliph, Mu'awiyah, utilized the shipyards to build a fleet for the invasion of Cyprus and to attack North Africa. Under Muslim rule in the next four centuries, Akko flourished and the port was a busy centre of trade.

Akko was taken by the Crusaders under King Baldwin I in 1104. His siege was supported from the sea by an Italian fleet from Genoa. By that time, Jerusalem was already in Crusader hands. But the struggle between the Christians and the Muslims for the control of the Holy Land was to be long and bitter. Akko was re-captured by the Muslims under Saladin in 1187. He was the most skilful of all the Islamic generals, and his capture of Akko was part of a campaign leading to the recapture of Jerusalem itself. The Holy City had been in Crusader hands for eighty-eight years, and the fall of Jerusalem to the forces of Saladin came as a great shock which was felt throughout Europe.

Four years later, Akko was retaken for the Crusaders by Richard Coeur de Lion of England, and Philip Augustus of France. Richard's main purpose was to retake Jerusalem, but it was a task which proved too difficult for his forces. At that time, Akko was renamed Acre. Since Jerusalem was in Islamic hands, Acre became the capital city of the Crusader kingdom. Fleets from Genoa, Venice and other Italian ports supplied Acre with provisions, and colonies of Italians lived in the city. They also took advantage of the port to expand trade with the east. The city had reverted to its traditional role as a trading port. The Knights and the Order of St Lazarus all had their quarters at Acre. The population increased and the city prospered.

Today, the city is once more called Accho — the original name. There are broad streets and modern buildings. Yet a visit to the Old City at Accho reminds the visitor of the long and complex history of the place. The remains of buildings from many periods can be seen. But usually the buildings have been altered by later inhabitants and utilized for different purposes. In 1291, the complete destruction of Acre by the forces of Islam marked the end of the Crusader kingdom. For three centuries, the city was deserted. Then, with the coming of the Ottoman empire, the city was once more developed as a fortress and trading port.

QUESTIONS FOR DEBATE

1. Can you suggest reasons why Acre played an important part in the Crusades?
2. Why did the recapture of Jerusalem by Saladin shock the Europeans?

Montfort   (4 mins)

The remains of a great Crusader castle called Montfort stand on a high narrow ridge in the hills overlooking the northern part of the coastal plain of the Holy Land. It was first built in the twelfth century and was called Castellum Novum Regis — the 'new castle of the king'. The ruins are the largest in western Galilee, and stand about nine miles from the sea at a height of about a thousand feet. The castle was built on several levels on the crest of the ridge and there are extremely steep slopes on either side of the ruins. It was built by a French count called Joscelin de Courtenay and, in Crusader times, it was linked by a local road to the port at Akko. But access to the site has always been very difficult and it is now only possible to approach the remains of the castle by foot.

When the Muslims captured Akko in 1187, they also took this fortress. It was reconquered by the Crusaders in 1192. The castle came into the hands of the Knights of the Teutonic order in 1228. The German knights enlarged it and used it as a treasury and a repository for their records. In such an inaccessible position, it was admirable for the purpose. The treasurer of the order always served as governor. The fortress was renamed Starkenberg by its German masters. In 1266, the castle, now called Montfort, was besieged unsuccessfully by the Muslims. It was only in 1271 that they managed to take it. After the knights had surrendered, they were allowed safe conduct by the Muslims to bring both themselves and their treasury to Acre. Montfort has been deserted ever since, and its inaccessibility has ensured that the walls have not been quarried for other buildings. It is a ruin in remarkably good condition, and can tell us a great deal about the ideas and the methods of the Crusaders.

The elongated plan of the fortress at Montfort reflects the shape of the ridge itself. The easiest point of attack was from the top of the ridge where a narrow saddle came down. To avoid this, the builders dug two deep moats into the rock at this point and a thick wall was erected below. The defences consisted of curtain walls and square towers. An oval-shaped keep was built in the highest part of the castle. Underneath the keep was a large cistern to ensure a plentiful store of water.

Lower down on the crest of the ridge were dwellings, a kitchen and the workshops of armourers. The remains of a winepress have been found near the kitchen. Pottery jars of various kinds have been discovered in the remains of the kitchen, and bits of armour in the armoury. The chapel and an open, paved area stood lower down on the ridge, below the dwellings and the workshops. They separated the public from the domestic buildings. The chapel was divided into a nave and two aisles. Fragments of stained glass were found on the floor of this chapel.

The governor's residence was next to the chapel and below that was a large, square ceremonial hall used for the meetings and ceremonies of the Teutonic Order. An elaborate roof in this hall was supported by finely-worked octagonal pillars. Underneath the ceremonial hall was a vaulted dungeon. Alongside the hall was a square tower. Many of the walls at Montfort have collapsed, and this is the only tower to remain standing at its original height. It affords spectacular views of the surrounding countryside. Below the fortress, on the banks of the small brook in the ravine below, can be found the remains of a farm and a dam used in Crusader times. The farm was a large, two-storied building which could also be used as a first line of defence.

Although it is a long and difficult trek to visit the remains of this fortress, Montfort does afford the visitor who makes the journey a remarkable insight into the ideas and the methods of the Crusaders. They were great military architects and engineers, capable of elaborate fortifications on almost impossible sites. But they treated the Holy Land as if they were dealing with a European country. So long as they had built a fortress to dominate the countryside, they believed themselves secure against all dangers. Yet history proved them wrong. Even a castle as difficult to take as Montfort was not capable of keeping the Holy Land in Crusader hands. The Muslims were closer to the hearts and minds of the local population.

QUESTIONS FOR DEBATE

1. Why was Montfort useful as a treasury?
2. Can you suggest reasons why the ideas of the native people of the Holy Land were important at the time of the Crusades?

The Bible

Origen   (5 mins)

Origen was born at Alexandria in Egypt towards the end of the second century A.D. Alexandria was the most important city of the eastern Mediterranean at the time, second only to Rome in the empire. There was a great library which contained, so it is said, fifty thousand books. People of many origins lived there, and there was a large Jewish community. The city was also a flourishing port and centre of trade. Alexandria was graced with broad streets and elegant classical buildings. Today, Egypt is largely a Muslim country, but in Origen's time this city, founded by Alexander the Great and named after him, was a centre of Christianity.

Yet it was dangerous to be a Christian in the Roman Empire of Origen's time. Lucius Septimus Severus was emperor. He had no sympathy with the Christians and, under him, many of them were persecuted for their beliefs. When Origen was about seventeen, his father Leonidas was arrested and put in prison. Origen's fiery spirit was roused. He longed to go out into the streets to complain about his father's arrest. He said that he did not care if he was killed. What could be better than that he should be martyred for the Christian faith? Origen's mother begged him not to invite such a catastrophe. Then, when he persisted, she was obliged to hide his clothes so that he could not leave the house. Soon after, Leonidas was beheaded. His property was taken by the state. He left a wife and seven sons.

Origen became a great scholar. He not only studied the Bible and the Christian religion. He also took a great interest in the writings of the ancient Greek philosophers. And he pursued knowledge wherever he could find it. After the persecutions of the Christians had died down in Alexandria, he began the work of giving instructions about the faith to new converts. And he wrote a series of important books about the Christian religion. During this period in his life he also made long journeys − to Rome, to Arabia, to Syria, to the Holy Land. Because of his reputation, he was invited to preach at the churches he visited on his travels. Demetrius, the bishop of Alexandria, disapproved. It was the beginning of a long dispute between Origen and the bishop. In about 220 A.D. matters came to a head.

Bishop Demetrius had Origen condemned at the synod of Alexandria. The outcome was that Origen was banished to Caesarea, in those days an important Christian centre on the coast of the Holy Land.

Origen had started his study of the Hebrew language while he was still living at Alexandria. Very few people of the time, apart from Jewish scholars, had any knowledge of Hebrew. The language of the Old Testament had not been spoken by ordinary people for centuries. In Jesus' time two centuries earlier, everybody in the Holy Land spoke Aramaic. They also spoke Greek. Greek was the universal language of the ancient world. For the sake of those Jews who could not understand the Hebrew, the Old Testament had been translated into Greek in the third century B.C. The translation was called the Septuagint. And since the Christians also could not understand Hebrew, it was the Greek Septuagint which was read at the Christian services.

Origen studied Hebrew because he was anxious that the Christians should have a knowledge of the Old Testament in the original language. He realized that a translation is never quite as good as the original. But he also knew that it would be difficult for large numbers of his fellow Christians to learn a dead language. He decided that he would supply his fellow Christians with a book containing as much information as possible about the Hebrew Old Testament. The result was Origen's *Hexapla*, begun at Alexandria and completed at Caesarea. In this book, he supplied six different versions of the Old Testament in parallel columns. First, there was the Hebrew text. Alongside it was a copy of the Hebrew, but this time using the Greek alphabet. People who could not read the original Hebrew could discover the sound of it by reading this column. Alongside these first two columns, Origen wrote out four different Greek translations of the Old Testament. In all, he had written out the Old Testament six times!

No copy of Origen's *Hexapla* has survived. Indeed, it seems unlikely that there ever was more than one original copy. In his day, books were written out laboriously by hand, word by word. The scribes certainly copied from the *Hexapla*, but took only one of Origen's columns and copied that. Yet this turned out to be a work of great importance in the history of the Bible. Origen's original copy of the *Hexapla* was stored at the great Christian library in Caesarea. About a century and a half later, a scholar called St Jerome came to the Holy Land. He had been commissioned by the pope to make a translation of the Bible into Latin from the original languages. He visited the library at Caesarea and studied the work which Origen had carried out. The result was the Vulgate, the most famous of all the translations of the Bible.

QUESTIONS FOR DEBATE

1. Do you think that Origen was right to want the readers of the *Hexapla* to know the sound of the Hebrew?
2. Would you agree with Origen that a translation is never as good as the original?

The Lindisfarne gospels   (6 mins)

There is an interesting riddle written in Exeter in the tenth century:

READER

> An enemy ended my life, deprived me of my physical strength: then he dipped me in water and drew me out again, and put me in the sun, where I soon shed all my hair. After that, the knife's sharp edge bit into me and all my blemishes were scraped away; fingers folded me and the bird's feather often moved over my brown surface, sprinkling meaningful marks; it swallowed more wood dye, and again travelled over me leaving black tracks. Then a man bound me, he stretched skin over me and adorned me with gold; thus I am enriched by the wondrous work of smiths, wound about with shining metal.

What is this riddle about? It starts with 'an enemy ended my life'. This was the slaughter of a sheep or a calf and the removal of its skin. You have to understand that it is the finished object which is speaking in this riddle, and animal skin is part of it. When 'he dipped me in water and drew me out again' this was the tanning process. Without tanning, skins go hard and brittle. Then, according to the riddle, the hair side of the skin was cleaned off and fingers folded the product.

   Can you guess what the riddle is about? Well the first part is about the making of parchment – animal skin, tanned, cleaned, bleached in the sun, making a good material on which people can write. And that's exactly what happens next in the riddle: 'the bird's feather often moved over my brown surface'. Handwriting in the tenth century involved using a goose quill, and the riddle talks of the feather swallowing more 'wood dye' — meaning ink. But that's not the end of the riddle: 'a man bound me, he stretched skin over me and adorned me with gold'. I think the meaning of the riddle is now obvious. This was the way of making a book in the tenth century — quite clearly a very fine book. At the end it is 'wound about with shining metal'.

Nowadays we are used to books which have been printed, quired and bound. People have found many new ways of making books, and the modern techniques enable us to produce them more and more cheaply. The text of a book can now be written on a word-processor directly onto the screen. Only when the writer is satisfied with what he has written, is it then printed. But such techniques were certainly not available to the people of the past. Indeed, until about five hundred years ago, not a single book had been printed in Europe, nor had a technique for making paper been devised.

The book described in the riddle was very expensive. To make a book required the skins of a whole flock of sheep or a herd of calves. And then the words had to be copied out by hand, word by word. In the case of a large book, the work could take months, or even years to finish. And the penmen who produced such books were artists. Not only was the writing itself beautiful, but they illuminated their work, with gold leaf and colours often wrought in elaborate designs. If you were to own such a book today, it would be worth a fortune. But it was also worth a great deal of money when it was new.

One of the finest examples of such a book was written by Eadfrith, Bishop of Lindisfarne. He lived in a monastery on a small island off the Northumberland coast — called Holy Island. The patron saint of the monastery was Saint Cuthbert, and the book was written in his honour. Eadfrith's book took about two years to write and to decorate, between the years 696 and 698 A.D. Afterwards, it was bound in a leather cover by Ethelwald, bishop of the islanders. And an anchorite called Billfrith adorned the outside with gold and precious stones. Nowadays, it is preserved at the British Library in London. It is well worth seeing. Some of the pages are completely given over to elaborate decoration in reds and blues and golds. And some of the letters, too, are heightened with intricate designs. But why did Eadfrith and his colleagues go to such great trouble? To them, the words in the book were holy. This was a copy of the four gospels, Matthew, Mark, Luke and John.

The gospels were originally written in Greek. These days, many different translations of them are available. But in Eadfrith's day, there was only one version — in Latin. This was St Jerome's great translation of the Bible into Latin produced about three hundred years earlier. So far as the people of Western Europe were concerned, Jerome's Vulgate was the Bible. They knew no other version. Eadfrith copied and decorated the Latin words with loving care.

In the year 793 A.D., nearly a hundred years after Eadfrith had produced his book, the monastic community on Holy Island was suddenly invaded by the Vikings.

As the great scholar, Alcuin of York, said at the time, 'never before has such terror appeared in Britain as we have now suffered from a pagan race, nor was it thought that such an inroad from the sea could be made'. Other monasteries in Britain were suffering the same fate, and the monks who re-established the monastery on Holy Island felt themselves in permanent danger. At last, in the year 875 A.D., they left the island taking their precious possessions with them. Eadfrith's book was among them. For twelve years, they wandered hither and thither looking for a place of safety. It was planned, at one time, to go to Ireland. But, as they put out to sea, a great storm arose and waves swept over the ship. They felt that Saint Cuthbert disapproved and decided to turn back. At last, they settled in Chester-le-Street in County Durham.

Eadfrith and the monks who followed him were, of course, scholars. They could read and write, and they understood Latin, the language of the Bible. When Jerome called his translation the Vulgate, he meant everybody to read it. The word 'Vulgate' means 'the book of the people'. But since books were so expensive, few people in England had the opportunity to learn to read. And most people did not understand Latin. The everyday language of the time was an early form of English called Anglo-Saxon. If you were suddenly transported back to the seventh century when Eadfrith lived, you would not understand a word he said in his native language, even though modern English has descended from it.

But while Eadfrith's gospels were at Chester-le-Street, a priest called Aldred decided to add to the book. This is his explanation:

READER
                Eadfrith, bishop of Lindisfarne Church, originally wrote this book for God, and for Saint Cuthbert and − jointly − all the saints whose relics are in the island. And Ethelwald, Bishop of the Lindisfarne islanders, impressed it on the outside and covered it − as he well knew how to do. And Billfrith, the anchorite, forged the ornaments which are now on it on the outside and adorned it with gold and with gems and also with gilded-over silver − pure metal. And Aldred, unworthy and most miserable priest, glossed it in English between the lines with the help of God and Saint Cuthbert . . .

If you visit the British Library today, you can see not only the Latin of the Vulgate which Eadfrith copied and decorated but also the work of Aldred, the 'unworthy and most miserable priest'. Two hundred and fifty years after the book had been made, while the community was at Chester-le-Street, he wrote a translation of the Latin words into the English language of his day. The ordinary people of the time had two problems when it came to the Bible. They could not read, and they did not understand Latin. Aldred, at least, had solved one of those problems. It is the earliest surviving translation into English of any part of the Bible.

QUESTIONS FOR DEBATE

1. Can you think of ways in which the invention of printing has changed the way people think about books?
2. Why do you think Aldred called himself an 'unworthy and miserable priest'? Has the word 'miserable' changed its meaning?

Desiderius Erasmus translates the New Testament   (7 mins)

He was the greatest scholar in Europe. He wrote manuscripts in London, corrected them in Paris and published them in Switzerland. He lectured at Cambridge, spent time in Italy, hobnobbed with popes and kings. His name was Desiderius Erasmus. Yet his origins were humble enough. He was born at Rotterdam in Holland in about 1469, the illegitimate son of a priest. He and his brother were orphaned at an early age. Erasmus had a habit of claiming that the guardians who had been appointed over the two boys cheated them of money they should have inherited from their mother. And he said that he was obliged, against his will, to enter a monastery. Yet he clearly received a good education under the Brethren of the Common Life at Deventer. And among his schoolfellows was Adrian of Utrecht, one day to be pope.

    The scholars of Erasmus' time had inherited one great advantage from the Middle Ages. Since all scholars could read Latin, there were no language barriers to international scholarship. Yet the world was changing in Erasmus' time. The development of printing enabled books to be much more freely available than in the past. And an important change in attitude had come about with the rediscovery of the literature of ancient Greece and Rome. We call such writings 'the classics'. What did that word 'classics' mean? The classics were the writings taught in class. The classics of the Middle Ages were the books of the Latin Bible – called the Vulgate. It had been translated from the original Hebrew and Greek into Latin by St Jerome at the end of the fourth century. The Vulgate was taught and explained in the Mediaeval classrooms of Europe. But when people began to read once more the literature of the ancient Greeks and Romans – particularly the Greeks – it opened their eyes to a whole vista of new ideas. We call the period the Renaissance – the rebirth of learning.

    Until Erasmus' time, hardly anybody in western Europe could read Greek. But suddenly there was a new interest in a noble pagan literature, much of it written before the birth of Christ. In his education, Erasmus was introduced to such new interests. He joined an Augustinian monastery and, in 1492, he was ordained a priest. Although the monastery offered him opportunities for reading all kinds of literature, the monastic life hardly suited Erasmus. In order to escape, he became secretary to one of the bishops – an appointment he did not hold for long. From then on, Erasmus was a scholar wandering the countries of Europe, usually short of money.

In 1499, Erasmus accepted an invitation to visit England. He later spoke jokingly of the barbarity of the English weather and his dislike of English beer. Yet England fascinated Erasmus and he returned many times in the years that followed. He made friends with many of the famous English scholars of the time – men such as William Latimer and Thomas More. He also came in contact with the young prince, later to be King Henry VIII. But the most important development on this first visit to England was during a short stay in Oxford. He found that the scholar John Colet was teaching New Testament studies not from the Vulgate, but from a manuscript copy of the original Greek. Erasmus was inspired. He spent the next few months in France and in Holland assiduously learning Greek. Then, in a monastery library in Belgium in 1504, Erasmus found a book which pointed out many of the weaknesses of the Vulgate. Improvements and corrections could be made to Jerome's famous translation of the Bible. To Erasmus, it was a revelation.

Erasmus hurried back to England and proceeded to borrow any Greek manuscripts of the New Testament he could find. These he used to make himself a copy in Greek. But Erasmus did not stay anywhere for long. In the next few years he spent time as a teacher and scholar in Turin, Bologna, Venice, Padua, Rome. He then returned to England and lectured at Cambridge. He taught Greek and lectured on the letters of St Jerome. In 1514, he was in Basel in Switzerland, working on his own edition of the New Testament in Greek together with a new elegant Latin translation. For a thousand years, the Vulgate had been considered by the people of Europe to be the only version of the Bible. Now, at least so far as the New Testament was concerned, it was possible for the ordinary reader to go back to the original language.

Erasmus did not learn Hebrew, the original language of the Old Testament. His contribution was confined to the New Testament. Yet he saw that the time would come when scholars would go back to the original languages and would translate not into Latin, the language of scholarship, but into the languages spoken by the ordinary people. As he wrote in his 'Preface' to the New Testament:

READER

> I could wish that every man might read the Gospel and the Epistles of St Paul. Would that these were translated into each and every language so that they might be read and understood not only by Scots and Irishmen,

but also by Turks and Saracens . . . Would that the farmer might sing snatches of scripture at his plough, that the weaver might hum phrases of scripture to the tune of his shuttle, that the traveller might lighten with stories from scripture the weariness of his journey.

QUESTIONS FOR DEBATE

1. Why was Latin, the international language of scholarship, so useful to Erasmus?
2. Can you suggest reasons why Erasmus wanted the scriptures to be available to Turks and Saracens?

William Tyndale   (8 mins)

This story has many sources. At the beginning of the sixteenth century, Desiderius Erasmus, the greatest scholar in Europe, had published a copy of the New Testament in Greek, the original language. And he included with the Greek a new translation into elegant Latin. At Alcala, in Spain, a group of scholars had published the whole Bible in a number of languages, including both the original Hebrew and the Greek. Then, in 1521 at Wartburg Castle in what is now East Germany, Martin Luther began one of the most important works of his life — the translation of the Bible from the original languages into a free and lucid German.

Up to that time, so far as Western Europe was concerned, St Jerome's translation of the Bible into Latin in the fourth century was the Bible. Priests, bishops, even the Pope himself knew no other. For a thousand years, hardly anybody had thought it necessary to go back to the original languages. Then, in a great flurry of activity in the sixteenth century, scholars learnt Greek and Hebrew and began to supply the world with new translations from the original. Martin Luther was the first to make a translation into a modern European language of the time.

Wartburg Castle, though, was a retreat for Luther. This passionate and melancholy man was involved in a battle with the Church, and he refused to give in. He rejected many important teachings, developed his own ideas, and demanded a complete reformation. Luther aroused furious opposition. In England, King Henry VIII wrote a book against him, and was awarded a medal by the Pope for doing so. Have you noticed 'F.D.' on the coins you have in your pocket? What do those letters stand for? 'Defender of the Faith' — that was the medal awarded to King Henry VIII by the Pope. Wartburg Castle was a retreat for Luther because the new ideas led not only to new translations of the Bible, but to a new understanding of the Bible. It now seemed possible to disagree with the teachings of the Church.

There was at Oxford a man called William Tyndale. After taking his degree he moved to Cambridge, the university at which the great scholar, Erasmus, had lectured. At Cambridge, he translated a treatise by Erasmus called 'The Manual of the Christian Soldier'. It was the beginning of his work as a translator. In 1523, he visited Fulham Palace, the residence of the Bishop of London. He spoke to Cuthburt Tunstall who was bishop at the time. Tyndale said that he wanted to make a new English translation of the Bible. What Luther was doing for the German people, he would do for England. The idea was rejected.

That rejection was clearly a matter of policy. There was no objection within the Church to the idea of going back to the original languages. That had already been done. But translation into languages which ordinary people could understand was different — not to be welcomed. If Martin Luther was any kind of example, it could encourage people to interpret the Bible as they wished. It struck at the heart of the authority of the Church.

What did Tyndale do? He emigrated. In 1524, he settled at Hamburg, an independent city and one of the most important ports in Europe at the time. His decision to carry on with the translation had aroused opposition, and the work could be done with greater safety outside England. He translated Erasmus' edition of the Greek New Testament into English at Hamburg. The printing of copies began at Cologne in 1525. But even in Germany, nothing was easy for Tyndale. The local magistrates intervened, and the printing had to be completed at Worms. Of the six hundred copies which were printed, only two have survived. Tyndale's New Testament was circulated in England. But in 1528, an injunction went out prohibiting the importation of copies. Cardinal Wolsey, King Henry VIII, even Thomas More, roundly condemned the work.

Charles V was nephew to Catherine of Aragon, the first wife of King Henry VIII. He was King of Spain and Holy Roman Emperor. His ideal was an orderly Church within an orderly Christendom. His officers imprisoned Tyndale at a castle at Vilvorde near Brussels in 1535:

READER
> . . . if I am to remain here through the winter, you will request the commissionary to have the kindness to send me a warmer cap, for I suffer greatly from cold in the head, and am afflicted with a perpetual catarrh, which is much increased in this cell. A warmer coat also, for

this which I have is very thin; a piece of cloth too to patch my leg-
gings. But most of all, I beg and beseech your clemency that he will
kindly permit me to have the Hebrew Bible, Hebrew grammar and
Hebrew dictionary . . .

So wrote Tyndale in a letter. His physical discomfort concerned him, but the books
were what mattered most. His translation of the Old Testament was not, however,
to be completed. It is one of the most tragic stories in the history of the Bible.
On October 6th, 1536, he was strangled and burnt at the stake on the orders of
Charles V, the Holy Roman Emperor.

Why did Tyndale's translation arouse such fury? Because revolution was in the
air. Even the very words of his translation could be seen to imply great changes.
He used, for instance, the word 'senior' instead of 'priest', and the word 'congregations' instead of 'church'. But the most serious charge of all was that, in his other
writings, he supported the ideas of Martin Luther.

But even before Tyndale's death, things had begun to change in England. In
January 1533, Henry VIII married Anne Boleyn. But he was already married to
the Spanish princess, Catherine of Aragon. No divorce had been granted or pronounced. Desperate for an heir, after long wranglings with the Pope, the King
had suddenly taken the law into his own hands. And in doing so, he accidentally
promoted a reformation in England. The following May, Thomas Cranmer, newly
appointed Archbishop of Canterbury, pronounced the divorce. Henry was declared
head of the Church in 'this realm of England'. The man who had received a medal
from the Pope had become disillusioned.

Among the possessions which Queen Anne Boleyn, Henry's new wife, has left
us is a copy of the Bible in English. It can still be seen today at the British Library.
Tyndale may have been imprisoned, but the work went on. His disciple, Miles
Coverdale, used Tyndale's translation, Jerome's Vulgate and Martin Luther's German Bible as the basis for a complete translation. It was published in 1535, probably at Cologne, and it was dedicated to King Henry VIII. The very work which
the churchmen had condemned, and which Henry had gone to such lengths to pro-
hibit, had become a proud possession. Queen Anne Boleyn's copy of the Bible
in English shows how much things had changed.

QUESTIONS FOR DEBATE

1. Which were more important, the new translations or the ideas which came
out of them?
2. Why do you think the invention of printing was so important when it
came to new translations of the Bible?

Count Konstantin von Tischendorf   (7 mins)

The Old Testament was written in Hebrew, the language of the Jewish people. But after the conquests of Alexander the Great, Greek became the universal language of the ancient world. Even in the streets of Rome, Greek was spoken as much as Latin. In New Testament times, it was the obvious language in which to spread the ideas of the new religion called Christianity. All the documents of the New Testament were written in Greek. The early Christians also used a version of the Old Testament translated from Hebrew into Greek. It is called the Septuagint.

But in the long history of the Bible, the languages people spoke kept on changing. By the fourth century, Latin had become the universal language of western Europe. St Jerome translated the Bible from the original Hebrew and Greek into Latin at the end of the fourth century. Much of the work was done when he was head of a monastery at Bethlehem in the Holy Land. His translation was called the 'Vulgate' − the book of the people.

But by the Middle Ages, Latin had developed into other languages − French, Italian, Spanish and Portuguese. And in some countries − Britain for instance − languages like English, not derived from Latin, had also developed. The western Church, centred on Rome, continued to use the Latin of the Vulgate long after the new languages had come into existence. The Vulgate, originally the book of the people, had now become the book of the Church. Only scholars could read Latin. The continued use of Latin cut ordinary people off from the Bible itself. It was one of the causes of the Reformation. As part of the protest against Rome, translations into modern languages began to appear. Martin Luther's translation of the Bible into German, for instance, was published in 1534.

But the way the Bible was passed on was also made more complicated by the method of making copies. Before the invention of printing, every word had to be written out by hand − the work of professional scribes. These Bibles were written on parchment or papyrus. Parchment was made from the skins of sheep or goats, scraped, bleached and tanned. Papyrus, which could become very brittle after a time, was made from the stems of papyrus plants. The earliest books were made up in the form of long scrolls which could be rotated so that the pages could be read. Later parchment or papyrus books, rather like the books we have today, came into existence. We call such books codices, and a single ancient book of this type is called a codex.

Passing on the Bible, then, was no simple matter. As the centuries passed, scholars became aware that, very likely, many mistakes had been made by the scribes. The search for really ancient copies began. The earlier the copy, the less likelihood there was of mistakes. One of the most famous scholars to hunt for ancient copies was Count Konstantin von Tischendorf. He was born in Saxony. In 1824 at the age of nineteen, he went to the university at Leipzig and began his studies of the text of the New Testament — a task which was to take him the rest of his life.

Tischendorf had amazingly sharp eyesight. It became very useful when he studied an early codex at the national library in Paris. This was a copy of the Bible in Greek, handwritten in the fifth century. But the writing had been erased by a monk in the twelfth century, and the parchment had been re-used for other purposes. Here and there, it was possible to see the original writing. But many experts had tried to read it, without success. Thanks to his remarkable eyesight, Tischendorf succeeded in reading it. It was the beginning of his reputation as an expert on ancient texts of the Bible.

In the spring of 1844, Tischendorf went to Cairo and visited many of the ancient monasteries of Egypt and Libya. Everywhere, he asked if the monks had ancient manuscripts. He discovered that the monks did not look after their valuable ancient books. Very often, the books were left under piles of dust in remote and unfrequented rooms. Tischendorf saw many interesting manuscripts in these monasteries, but what he wanted was an early copy of the Bible.

The last place Tischendorf visited was the famous St Catherine's Monastery at the foot of Mount Sinai. It took him ten days of travelling through the desert to get there. To enter the monastery, he was pulled up by the monks to a doorway high in the wall. It was the only way in. As in the other monasteries, Tischendorf found that the books and manuscripts were neglected. But, after going through great piles of dusty parchments and papyri, he found what he had been looking for. Here was one of the earliest manuscripts in existence of part of the Septuagint — the Hebrew Old Testament translated into Greek. This had been handwritten in about 350 A.D. It was indeed an exciting find. But it took a great deal of bargaining with the monks before they would allow him to take away forty-three of the hundred and twenty-nine sheets of the manuscript. The rest he had to leave in the monastery.

In 1854, Tischendorf returned to St Catherine's monastery a second time. He wanted those other sheets. When he got there, things were much the same as on his first visit. The monks were welcoming, but not in the least helpful. And there was no sign of the priceless sheets. They seemed to have completely disappeared. At last, Tischendorf left to visit other monasteries, then went home to Leipzig without the rest of the codex. But he could not leave it at that. The thought tormented him. Either the monks had sold the other sheets, or they were still there.

Tischendorf returned to St Catherine's Monastery five years later. This time, he had the support of the Czar of Russia in his quest. The monks of St Catherine's had great respect for the Czar. But it made little difference. There was no sign of the parchments. Then, on the last day of his visit, he was invited by a young monk into his cell. There, in that cell, there were many more parchments than Tischendorf had ever imagined. Not only were there the missing sheets, but also a handwritten copy of the New Testament and two other early Christian books. Tischendorf's treasure hunt was over.

Today, the Codex Sinaiticus — so called because it was found at St Catherine's Monastery at the base of Mount Sinai — is in the British Library. Thanks to Tischendorf, scholars are able to compare this early copy of the Bible with other early copies. It was a rare find indeed.

QUESTIONS FOR DEBATE

1. Can you suggest reasons why the monks at St Catherine's Monastery took very little care of the manuscripts?
2. Why do scholars value the work done by Tischendorf?

The Scientists

Galileo   (6 mins)

The great Greek philosopher Aristotle lived between 384 and 322 B.C. As part of his philosophy, he thought of ways of explaining how everything in the universe works. He observed changes and occurences around him and, in a logical way, he built up a believable explanation of everything. His approach was based upon such simple ideas that they could be grasped by anybody. For nearly two thousand years after this time, people agreed that his theories seemed to fit the facts. But unfortunately Aristotle's theories were wrong. He believed, for instance, that a stone falls towards the earth because it is a part of the earth. It did not occur to him that the fall of the stone had anything to do with gravity. In Aristotle's view too, fire rises upwards because it is a part of the air — not because it is in the nature of heat to rise. Anyone today using Aristotle's theories to answer examination questions in Physics would get no marks.

The man who was, perhaps, most responsible for changing these ideas was an Italian named Galileo Galilei. He began his studies in the 1580s. Strangely enough, he admired Aristotle and had no intention of undermining his theories. He tried to do no more than correct one or two mistakes he had discovered. But as he continued, Galileo discovered larger and larger errors. Also, under Aristotle's system, there had been no practical science. Everything was to be explained by thinking about it. Galileo decided to test his theories by conducting experiments. This was something that people had not done before. In the work of Galileo, Aristotle's ideas were gradually experimented out of existence.

Galileo made discoveries about gravity. He studied acceleration, and formulated laws about floating objects. His new knowledge fundamentally opposed the laws of Aristotle, but his experiments were easy and entertaining for people to perform. After Galileo had published one of his books, people could disprove Aristotle in their own kitchens. Galileo did not attempt to create a new philosophy of life around his discoveries. He saw himself as being at the forefront of a great change in thinking. He believed that a new philosophy would come naturally as more was learnt.

Galileo invented the thermometer, the compass, and the pendulum clock. But he is best known for developing the telescope. This instrument was invented in Holland in 1608. By the following year Galileo had made one for himself and had substantially improved upon the design. In turning it upon the sky, once more he came across things which disproved Aristotle's ideas. Aristotle said that everything in the sky was perfect and that it had been placed there for human enjoyment. But Galileo saw mountains upon the moon. They proved that the moon is not perfectly round. He also realized that such mountains were not visible to the naked eye — so that without a telescope humans could not enjoy them. Galileo's observations were not, however, universally welcomed. The followers of Aristotle were angered at his discoveries, but more importantly so were the leaders of the Church.

Galileo accepted the idea of the solar system — first suggested by Nicholas Copernicus in 1543. For the first time, scientists began to see that the earth is a planet in orbit around the sun. But now the leaders of the Church decided that belief in the solar system went against the teachings of the Bible. In the book of Job for instance, God is described as 'he . . . who shakes the earth out of its place, and its pillars tremble; who commands the sun, and it does not rise'. The biblical writers clearly believed that the earth stands at the centre of the universe. In 1616 the Inquisition set up by the Church decided that the idea of a fixed sun and a moving earth was 'foolish and absurd'. Galileo was forbidden to hold such views any more.

But Galileo continued his work. Another of his books was published in which the traditional idea of the universe was compared unfavourably with the concept of the solar system. The Pope was very angry, and Galileo was summoned before the Inquisition in 1633, at nearly seventy years of age. It was ordered that none of his books could be printed or reprinted, and that he was to be a virtual prisoner for the remainder of his life. This ruling affected Galileo deeply as he was a devout Christian. But he knew that he was in the right and he died with a clear conscience in 1642.

QUESTIONS FOR DEBATE

1. Why was the conducting of experiments such an important step forwards?
2. Does modern science contradict the teachings of the Bible?

William Harvey   (6 mins)

For many centuries people had puzzled over the nature of blood. The ancient philosophers tried to decide why there is blood in the bodies of living animals. The people of the Old Testament came to the conclusion that the blood is the life of the animal. It explains why meat eaten by the Jews was drained of blood. They did not wish to eat an animal's life. When William Harvey began his revolutionary work on the circulation of the blood early in the seventeenth century, the ideas about blood common at the time were still based on the work of Galen, physician to the emperor of Rome in the first century A.D.

Galen had made great leaps forward in the field of medicine. But he also held back progress for over a thousand years. His theories were so simple and believable that it was not thought worthwhile to seek alternatives. Galen divided the body and its blood supply into three parts. The blood itself he saw as flowing up and down the veins in a tide-like movement. The first part of the body was concerned with growth. Food would work its way down towards the liver where it would be made into blood and flow up to the left side of the heart. The second part of the body, based in the right side of the heart, was concerned with the manufacture of courage, anger, personality and body heat. Here the blood flowed through the arteries via the lungs. For the third section of the body, some of the blood worked its way up to the head and brain where it was involved with the growth of the intellect, sensation and movement. The heart was much more than just a bodily organ. In Galen's theory it was involved with every aspect of personality.

This theory overshadowed all others until the work of William Harvey. Yet small steps were made before this time. In 1543, the publication of a book by Vesalius gave the first complete and reasonably accurate account of the human body. Even more important was the discovery made by Hieronymous Fabricius in 1574 that there are valves in the veins of the human body. This discovery is particularly important in the work of Harvey as he was taught by Fabricius at his college in Padua. Harvey was regarded at college as being very good at devising experiments, many of which put him ahead of his teachers in understanding. Experiments were not really a part of the physician's course at that time. Here, Harvey himself gives his own ideas on the subject:

READER
> Careful observation is needed in every discipline... one's own experience is to be relied upon, not that of someone else.

This was the basis of Harvey's success. Fabricius showed his students his great discovery of the valves in the veins and informed them that their purpose was to slow down the flow of blood through the body. This explanation was not good enough for Harvey. He looked deeper into the subject, only to discover that they act in such a way as to stop the blood flowing back through the veins. It meant that, instead of blood ebbing and flowing through the body – a view which man had held for over a thousand years – blood must flow in one direction.

The discovery of the circulation of the blood led to fundamental changes in the way in which doctors were to work in the future. In 1628, at the age of fifty, Harvey published his first book in which his conclusions were put before the public for the first time. Instead of the philosophical interpretations of Galen, Harvey saw the human body and its workings as essentially mechanical. He saw the heart as a pump and observed the circular movement of the blood through the body. The heart contains four separate chambers called auricles and ventricles. The auricles, he noticed, received blood, whilst the ventricles pumped it out. The circulation around the body was very simple. The purpose of the blood is to supply oxygen to all parts of the body. This oxygen is collected from the lungs. From there the blood passes to the left auricle, thence to the left ventricle where it is pumped through the whole body and back again to the right auricle, the right ventricle, and once more to the lungs. 'I am obliged to conclude,' said Harvey, 'that in animals the blood is driven round a circuit with an unceasing, circular sort of movement'.

Every major change in human thought has come about slowly because people are unwilling to accept change. Harvey's ideas met with considerable resistance. One particular doctor of the time argued that, as people had got on very well all these years without the circulation of the blood, there was no such thing. The opposition to Harvey's discoveries, though, had very little ammunition. He became one of the leading physicians of his day, personal doctor to King James I and later to Charles I. It was unfortunate that he was so closely attached to a king who was destined to involve his country in civil war.

Harvey was probably not made president of the College of Physicians because of his attachment to Charles I. More serious, as a part of the Royal household when Charles was finally taken by Cromwell's troops in 1644, Harvey was taken as well. But Harvey was still admired by many people. He was not directly involved with the war. Throughout he had continued with his work and had not become involved in the fighting. Accounts differ as to how he was treated by the Roundheads. According to one story he was set free with no blame attached. According to another he was fined £2,000 for his involvement with the king. What is known is that after Charles' execution in 1649, as a member of the Royalists, Harvey's house was looted and many of his medical notes were burnt and lost forever.

Because of this and because of his attachment to Charles I, Harvey was greatly distressed by the Commonwealth period. He is reported to have said:

READER

> . . . were I not refreshed by the comfort of my studies and the recollection of things I have once observed, I (should) have no reason for wishing to live any longer.

Unfortunately he did not live long enough to see the return of the monarchy in 1660, but he did die recognized once more as the greatest physician of the age. By the time of his death in 1656 he had amassed a fortune of £20,000 — a considerable sum of money in those days. It shows how highly he was regarded by his contemporaries. William Harvey began man's understanding of the nature of the human body.

QUESTIONS FOR DEBATE

1. What reasons can you suggest as to why the people of the Old Testament believed that the blood is the life of the animal?
2. What was Harvey's most important discovery?

Gilbert White's tortoise   (4 mins)

Gilbert White was a clergyman in the eighteenth century who worked most of his adult life in the little village of Selborne in Hampshire. The tranquil country way of life suited him admirably, and he spent much of his time in the garden which he loved. In 1751, he began to keep a calendar of all the most important events which took place in the garden during the course of the year. By this time, he was experimenting with new strains of plants and with new methods of cultivation. They are all noted down with meticulous care in *The Garden Kalendar*. He was one of the first people in Britain to experiment with vegetables which, in the eighteenth century, were new to people — such foods as sea-kale, wild rice, maize and potatoes. It was the beginning of an interest which was later to be extended outside the garden itself. In 1768, he had begun *The Naturalist's Journal* in which his entries included anything and everything which took his interest.

Less than a year after the very first manned balloon flight, Gilbert White writes in his diary:

READER

> Sept. 4, 1784 — My Neph: Edmd White launched a balloon on our down, made of soft, thin paper; and measuring about two feet and a half in length and 20 inches in diameter. The buoyant air was supplyed at the bottom by a plug of wool, wetted with spirits of wine, and set on fire by a candle. The air being cold & moist this machine did not succeed well abroad: but in Mr Yalden's staircase it rose to the ceiling, and remained suspended as long as the spirits continued to flame, & then sunk gracefully. These Gent: made the balloon themselves. This small exhibition explained the whole balloon affair very well: but the position of the flame wanted better regulation; because the least oscillation set the paper on fire.

Gilbert White loved to understand why things worked, particularly in nature. On March 17th, 1780, he acquired a tortoise called Timothy from Mrs Snooke, one of his neighbours. He immediately began a close and careful study of the animal. Unfortunately for Timothy, this was during the tortoise's hibernation:

READER

> March 17, 1780 . . When dug out of its hybernaculum, it resented the insult by hissing.

From then onwards, Gilbert White kept a careful watch on Timothy, observing many strange habits which others perhaps had missed. All kinds of details were noted — how he went to sleep at 'four o'clocke p.m.' on April 22nd, and how he tipped himself against the garden wall in order to catch more of the sun as the weather turned colder. Gilbert White's enthusiasm both for observation and for experimentation was aroused when there was such a peculiar creature as a tortoise round the house:

READER

> July 1, 1780 — We put Timothy into a tub of water, & found that he sunk gradually, & walked on the bottom of the tub: he seemed quite out of his element, & was much dismayed. This species seems not to be amphibious . . .

Timothy seems to have survived this treatment well enough, and Gilbert White's entries continue unabated:

READER

> Sept. 17, 1780 — When we called loudly thro' the speaking-trumpet to Timothy, he does not seem to regard the noise.

Remarkably, the debate as to whether or not a tortoise can hear continues to this day. His rather crude experiment of two hundred years ago was the first in a long line of enquiries, many of them much more sophisticated, which have not as yet resolved this problem.

   Gilbert White is important, not as a great scientist who presented the world with startling new discoveries, but rather as an ordinary man who wished to work things out for himself. His purpose was to have a greater knowledge of nature, and of the way in which things work. He was a clergyman who lived at a time when people marvelled at the idea of God as a supreme mathematician and designer. They saw God as the creator of a solar system; planets in orbit around the sun working on mathematical principles. They understood God as having a reason for everything in his creation. In such a climate of opinion, it was natural for a country parson to study the plants, the animals — everything that surrounded him. But it is likely that Timothy did not always enjoy the attention he received.

QUESTIONS FOR DEBATE

1. Does it really matter if scientists never find out whether tortoises can hear — or is knowledge for its own sake important?
2. Do you disapprove of experiments on animals?

Isambard Kingdom Brunel   (4 mins)

Isambard Kingdom Brunel was born at Portsea on 9th April, 1806, the son of a well respected engineer. From a very early age, he was fascinated by engineering. His interest was probably sparked off when, as a small boy, he watched his father at work. It was from his father that the young Brunel learnt geometry and drawing. Throughout school and college it became clear that he had a talent for these skills and it seemed only natural that, when he began his career, he joined his father's business.

For many years the possibility had been discussed of boring a tunnel under the river Thames. In 1825 the task of digging this tunnel was given to the Brunels. This was to be Isambard's first important work and he put his heart and soul into it. With a revolutionary digging device designed by his father, the tunnel to stretch from Rotherhithe to Limehouse was begun. By 1826, Isambard's unstoppable enthusiasm had earned him the position of resident engineer on the project, and he was often down the tunnel for twenty-four hours at a time. But things did not go well. After the tunnel had flooded for the second time killing six men and injuring Brunel himself, the work was abandoned. The tunnel was not finished until 1843. But it can still be seen today as a part of the London underground railway system.

Brunel's injuries took some time to heal, and he moved to Bristol to convalesce. It was in and around Bristol that he began to work on his own account for the first time. He entered a competition to design a bridge over the Clifton gorge, some seven hundred feet wide and two hundred feet deep. His revolutionary design for a suspension bridge won the competition. But not enough money could be raised to build the bridge. He briefly spent some time in Sunderland designing docks on the River Wear but, although his designs were accepted, only smaller versions of his docks were built. He returned to Bristol. There, his ideas for improving the harbour were accepted. But they were carried out only half-heartedly. This was 1833 and it must have seemed to Brunel that nothing he designed would ever be finished.

It was around this time, though, that he put his name forward for a new railway project that was being considered. This was to be a massive undertaking – a rail link between Bristol and London. It was to be known as the Great Western Railway. To his surprise, Brunel was appointed. The 1820s and 30s had seen the birth of the railways. The art of building them was still very much in its infancy. Before any work was done on the line, Brunel went on a two year survey, trying to work out the best route. Steam trains were not good at climbing gradients. The line would have to be as level as possible. Brunel also had to take into account the nature of the soil, through which towns the line would pass, and who owned the land on which the railway would be built.

But when the building of the line was begun, Brunel's work was by no means over. The construction of the Great Western Railway required a whole multitude of skills which Brunel had in abundance. His assistant, Clark wrote:

READER

> . . . every structure on the Great Western, from the smallest culvert up to the Brent viaduct and Maidenhead bridge was entirely, in all its details, from his own designs.

Despite this mammoth task, he was also involved at the same time with revolutionizing steam shipping. And he was finally beginning work on the Clifton suspension bridge. This may explain why the line of the Great Western Railway was not very good when it was first opened. The rails were not laid well and the locomotives were faulty. But such problems were soon ironed out.

Brunel's involvement in steam shipping came as a result of his desire to lengthen the Great Western route all the way to America. If he could design a ship to sail directly from Bristol to New York this could be done. But no such ship had ever been designed. It was thought that such a vessel would have to be enormous because it had to hold enough coal for such a voyage. This was in 1835, the very year work was finally begun on the Clifton suspension bridge. But no workload seemed too much for Brunel. He kept all three projects under way.

Several competitors were also busy trying to build a ship which could travel the Atlantic under steam. When things came to a head, it was a race which Brunel seemed to have lost. A fire aboard his ship, the 'Great Western', allowed a rival ship, the 'Sirius' to sail for America first. It left on 28th March 1837, a full twenty-six days before the 'Great Western' was ready. The 'Sirius' arrived in New York to a rapturous welcome. But when the 'Great Western' arrived that same afternoon, it was obvious that Brunel had really won the day. His ship was much better than the 'Sirius' in every way. Immediately, he began to design a revolutionary new ship to be called the 'Great Britain'. Twice the size of the 'Great Western', it was to have an iron hull and a screw propeller instead of paddles. This ship was finished in 1843 and changed ideas on ship design thereafter. Meanwhile, work on the Clifton bridge had been stopped once more.

This was a time when the growth of the railways was going ahead at great speed. Nobody had really conceived of how important they might become, but there was a major sticking point. Brunel's line had been built using broad gauge tracks, whereas other lines used a narrow gauge. It would eventually be narrow gauge which would cover the country, but the arguments raged for many years, Brunel insisting that broad gauge tracks were the best. Meanwhile his work continued with the building of Paddington and Bristol stations.

Brunel's last great idea was the construction of a steam ship that might sail all the way to Australia. This was to be the largest ship ever built and was to be called the 'Great Eastern'. It had to be built parallel to the river because it was too large to be launched bow first. In 1857, Brunel had to face the problem of how he was going to launch the ship sideways. He tried and failed at the beginning of November, and again in the middle of the month. At last, high tide on 3rd January, 1858 saw the ship floating free. But by this time, Brunel's health was failing. And his constant worries about the 'Great Eastern' proved too much for him. The day before its first sailing he collapsed. From his sick-bed, Brunel heard that one of the great boilers on board had burst. This news was too much for him and six days later he died.

The 'Great Eastern' never really lived up to Brunel's expectations. It was too far ahead of its time. The technology of his day was not really good enough. The ship did, however, achieve fame. It was the ship which laid the first transatlantic telegraph cable. The 'Great Eastern' was finally broken up in the 1890s. Brunel's works, though, still reveal him as one of the greatest engineers the world has ever seen. His Clifton suspension bridge was finally finished as a tribute to his memory.

QUESTIONS FOR DEBATE

1. Do you think we should admire Brunel's single-mindedness?
2. Can you suggest reasons why the development of the railway system was so important?

Charles Darwin   (6 mins)

Charles Darwin was not a good scholar. He failed his course in medicine at Edinburgh university, and scraped through his exams at Cambridge when he moved there to prepare for a career as a clergyman. His main interests at the time were shooting, riding and hunting. But while he was at Cambridge he did strike up a friendship with John Stevens Henslow, Professor of Botany. Darwin had been fascinated by natural history from a very early age — although he had always regarded his enthusiasm as merely a hobby. He enjoyed botanical trips around Cambridge with Henslow, but always saw them as little more than a pleasant diversion from his more serious studies. But Henslow must have taken these interests seriously. In 1831, there was a vacancy for a naturalist aboard a ship going on a surveying voyage around the world. Henslow put Darwin's name forward.

Darwin was twenty-two, and had left college expecting to become a clergyman.

This was not because he was particularly religious, but because he needed a career. The church was a common choice at that time, and his father was anxious that he should settle down to useful employment. When he was offered the opportunity to work as a naturalist on this excursion, it was thought that the voyage would probably last from two to four years. At first, Darwin's father would not hear of it. Darwin appealed to his uncle Josiah Wedgewood, head of the famous pottery firm. With his help, Darwin's father was persuaded and he set off to meet the captain of H.M.S. Beagle.

Captain Robert Fitzroy was an intensely religious man. He wanted to take a naturalist aboard the Beagle so that certain passages of the Bible might be proven beyond doubt. He was particularly interested in finding evidence to support the biblical stories of the Creation and of Noah's Ark. The young Darwin was only too happy to support these aims. This was an age when people accepted every word of the Bible quite literally, and Darwin was no exception. The official work of the voyage was principally to chart the little known coastline of Patagonia in South America.

The small, cramped ship set off after many delays on 27th December, 1831. Darwin was seasick almost immediately and was to remain so, to a greater or lesser extent, throughout the remainder of the voyage. But at each stop along the way, Darwin began to collect, note, record and observe. In his enthusiasm, he was determined to miss nothing. In the tropical rain forest, whilst the ship was moored at Rio de Janeiro, Darwin encountered a greater variety of life than he had ever seen before, and he began to observe the nature of animals in their natural habitat. To prey and be preyed upon seemed to be how animals were meant to live. He saw moths disguised as scorpions, insects that looked like twigs, all kinds of predators attacking all kinds of prey. Even humans were not exempt from the basic laws of nature: 'I was told before leaving England,' wrote Darwin, 'that after living in slave countries all my opinions would be altered; the only alteration I am aware of is forming a much higher estimate of the negro character.'

As they began to study the unmapped coastline of Patagonia, Darwin continued his observations wherever the Beagle stopped. On a desolate section of coastline, around four hundred miles south of Buenos Aires, at a place called Punta Alta, Darwin came across some enormous fossilized bones. Very little was known at this time about prehistoric animals, and to Darwin the discovery was very exciting. At this place he came across the fossils of many different creatures, but what struck him most was the resemblance of many of them to their living counterparts. The giant sloth or armadillo and the prehistoric elephant were obviously related in some close way to the living creatures of the present. Yet what was immediately obvious was that the present inhabitants of South America were very different from the ones God had originally created for this part of the world. Far from lasting a mere seven days, the Creation seemed to have taken millions of years.

Darwin's next major discovery was in the Andes mountains. Here, he saw fossilized sea shells, proof that the land at this point had once been submerged. Once again it seemed that the Bible's view of Creation in seven days was being disproved. Captain Fitzroy was deeply opposed to the conclusions which Darwin drew from his observations. He believed Darwin was becoming a heretic. After all, the discovery of the remains of the sea shells seemed to be evidence of the Great Flood described in the Bible. But Darwin was no longer convinced by the Bible's interpretation of events, and further evidence was to come.

At Valdivia in Chile they were caught in the middle of a massive earthquake. Before their very eyes the land rose a few more feet out of the sea. If it could rise that much in a matter of seconds, why not thousands of feet over millions of years? It was at the Galapagos Islands in the Pacific that Darwin's ideas started to take a definite form. Here, between islands very close together, he noticed significant differences in the forms of life. Many plants and animals were unique, not only to the group of islands, but to each individual island. Darwin observed one species of finch which on one island had developed a strong beak for cracking nuts and seeds, whilst on another the same kind of bird had developed a smaller beak for eating insects. It was clear that successive generations had adapted themselves to their individual conditions.

Bringing together all of his observations much later in life, Darwin was to call this the 'survival of the fittest' or 'natural selection'. His theories, formed upon this mission which lasted five years, were not to be published until 1859, some twenty-three years after his return. The delay was because his views were regarded as heretical. When it was published, his book, *The Origin of the Species* inevitably caused a great deal of controversy. But the evidence which Darwin had collected was there for anybody to see. Almost reluctantly, Darwin had been forced to change forever man's view of his world, of himself and, indeed, of the Bible. But it did not please everybody when it was said that, far from being created in the image of God, human beings probably shared ancestors with the ape.

QUESTIONS FOR DEBATE

1. Do Darwin's theories completely undermine the teachings of the Bible?
2. Why were Darwin's ideas so important in the nineteenth century?

Albert Einstein   (6 mins)

Albert Einstein was born at Ulm in Germany on 14th March, 1879. The following year, the family moved to Munich where his father and his uncle set up a small engineering works. As a child he seemed a slow learner. He did not talk until he was three and, at primary school, his teachers did not regard him very highly. Yet later in life he told people that, even before his school days had begun, he remembered being fascinated by a compass. It was the beginning of his lifelong interest in physics. By the time he reached secondary school he was far ahead of the rest of the pupils in mathematics and physics. He taught himself such subjects outside school hours. Yet he left school at the age of fifteen with no diploma and with poor grades in history, geography and languages.

Einstein's parents were Jewish, but they did not bother much with the customs and the lifestyle of their inherited religion. As a child, he reacted against this and became for a while intensely religious. But by the time he was twelve years old and had become deeply interested in science, his attitude towards the Jewish religion changed. He could not reconcile the two worlds of religion and science. So he became an atheist.

In 1905, when he was twenty-six, he published an astonishing number of new scientific writings all in the same year. They were to make his reputation as a scientist. Einstein was important because he questioned what people called 'common sense'. If, for instance, a boat is travelling at 20 miles per hour down a river which flows at 10 miles per hour, how fast is it actually going? Common sense says that is is travelling at 30 miles per hour − the speed of the boat added to the speed of the water. In fact, so Einstein discovered, it travels at 29.99999999999999866 miles per hour. This may not seem very important, but when the speeds are much greater the effect is also much greater. If, for instance, we add 20 billion millimetres per second to 20 billion millimetres per second, the total is not 40 billion millimetres per second but 27.3 billion millimetres per second. Mother Nature is not bound by what seem to us the rules of common sense. These observations were part of Einstein's theory of relativity, first suggested in an essay when he was only sixteen years old.

In the summer of 1914, Einstein's wife and two sons went on holiday to Switzerland, while he stayed at home in Berlin where he was a lecturer. World War I broke out while they were away. They could not return and the family was broken up. Einstein hated the war and was an outspoken critic of German militarism. At this time, he became a pacifist. But he was mainly occupied during the wartime in perfecting his theory of relativity. And when the war came to an end, he was suddenly famous. The Royal Society in London recognized and proclaimed the importance of his work. Einstein became a celebrity − accepted as the most important physicist of the age.

His marriage did not survive the wartime separation from his wife and he was divorced in 1919. He remarried, and lived with his new wife Elsa and her two daughters from a previous marriage. In between the wars, he was much in demand as a lecturer and travelled widely throughout the world. In 1921, he received the Nobel prize. During this period, he began his quest for a universal law within which all physics could be accommodated. He spent the rest of his life trying to establish it — and failed.

In between the wars, hatred of the Jews was building up in Germany, encouraged by the rise of Hitler. Although Einstein did not accept the Jewish religion, he still regarded himself as a Jew and publicly supported the Jewish cause. In 1933, soon after Hitler became chancellor of Germany, Einstein renounced his German citizenship and moved to the United States of America. He became a member of the School of Mathematics at the Institute of Advanced Study in Princeton. At this time, Einstein horrified his pacifist friends by publicly giving up his pacifist beliefs. He was so convinced that Hitler was preparing for war that he tried to encourage the other countries of Europe to attack Germany. His warnings were ignored, and there were fears for his safety.

Although Einstein's scientific work in the later part of his life did not produce any new results, he was still regarded as an important figure in the world of science. He corresponded with some of the most famous people of his day. Occasionally, his comments attracted the attention of the world press. After the explosions of the atomic bomb at Hiroshima and Nagasaki which brought the Second World War to a close, for instance, Einstein advised that nations 'should submit to the binding authority necessary for world security'. In his closing years, he was a grand old man, a famous scientist and citizen of the world. Yet political leaders took little notice. Einstein died in 1955.

QUESTIONS FOR DEBATE

1. Suggest reasons for Einstein's interest in science.
2. What did Einstein mean when he said, 'Politics are for a moment; an equation is for eternity'?

The British

Battle Abbey   (5 mins)

On the grounds where the remains of Battle Abbey now stand, there took place the best remembered conflict in the history of England — the Battle of Hastings in 1066. Harold, earl of Wessex, had been accepted as the new King of Anglo-Saxon England in succession to Edward the Confessor whose marriage had been childless. But William, duke of Normandy, was Edward's cousin once removed, and believed that he had a claim to the English throne.

It had all started badly for William. No doubt it had been his intention to sail to the English coast and to capture the Isle of Wight. It would have given him a base for his campaign. But severe weather had kept the Norman ships in harbour for a month, and then a westerly gale had forced some of them up channel. He had lost shipping at sea. The waiting had not suited his troops. Morale was low.

On September 25th, 1066 Harold of England defeated the army of the King of Norway who had invaded in the north. The Norwegian army included Harold's exiled brother Tostig. The battle took place at Stamford Bridge near York. On September 27th, William finally set sail for England, and the following day he took the towns of Hastings and Pevensey on the south coast. He was encamped on a narrow strip of land between the sea and the great forest of Andred. William's invasion involved Harold and his troops in a long march south. The Saxon army finally appeared out of the forest on October 13th, surprising the Normans. But it was towards evening, and instead of pushing on to retake Hastings, Harold camped on a hilltop north of the Norman army.

The following day, William roused his troops before dawn and early in the morning they were deployed on the battle field. The two armies were roughly of equal size, and the morale of the Saxons was high after their victory at Stamford Bridge. William attacked the massed army of the Saxons with archers, with cavalry and with footsoldiers. But he saw his troops virtually swept off the field. It was only his energetic pursuit of fleeing Norman soldiers, and his determination to get them back into the battle, which saved the day. In the Bayeux tapestry which records the events of the battle, there is a picture of William driving his troops back against the Saxons at the end of his spear. Towards nightfall, Harold was killed and the Saxon army gave up.

William had vowed to his troops before the battle that if God granted him victory, he would found a monastery 'for the salvation of you all, and especially those who fall'. But during the winter after the victory, William was extremely busy securing England into Norman hands. He was crowned king at Westminster Abbey on Christmas Day, 1066. It was some months before he came to fulfil his vow. He entrusted the task to William Faber, a monk from Marmoutier in Normandy. William instructed that the high altar of the new Battle Abbey should stand over the place where Harold had fallen. When Faber started the work of building on what he considered to be a better site, he was told to take it down and start again. William did not mince his words.

For nearly five hundred years, there were Benedictine monks at Battle Abbey — called 'black monks' because of the colour of their habits. The order of St Benedict was based on the rules laid down for the monks at Monte Cassino in Italy in the sixth century. Benedict's Rule consisted of a prologue and seventy-three chapters. The monks were to share a common life of poverty, chastity and obedience. Prayer was the chief task of a monk's life, and he took part in seven services a day. Some of the monks were among the most learned people in the land, and desks were provided for them in the cloisters of the abbey so that they could read or write.

Although the idea of the monastic life was that the monks should dedicate themselves entirely to God, life was far from simple in these great Mediaeval institutions. The monks met in the Chapter House each day, so that the business of the monastery could be discussed. That was followed by a reading of one of the chapters out of the Rule of St Benedict. It explains why the building was called the Chapter House. And the rules themselves went into considerable detail about what the monks were allowed to do. There was a Rule of Silence at the Abbey, although in the early days of the monastery, the monks could talk to each other in a room called the parlour, below the dormitory where they slept. The only language they were allowed to speak was Latin.

Nowadays, Battle Abbey is a ruin. Little remains of the great buildings which occupied the hilltop where Harold and his troops suffered defeat at the hands of William the Conqueror. The ruins remind the visitor of the doings of another King of England, Henry VIII. After breaking England away from the Papacy in 1533, Henry was determined to crush the power of the monasteries. In May, 1538, he sent his royal commissioners to seize Battle Abbey and its treasures. The Abbot and the monks were dismissed. The great church was deliberately smashed into a pile of rubble. What one King of England had built, another destroyed.

QUESTIONS FOR DEBATE

1. Why did William want the high altar of Battle Abbey to stand where Harold had died?
2. Why did the Mediaeval monasteries become very rich?

Margery Kempe   (5 mins)

The county of Norfolk comprises the flattest land in England. These days, thanks to modern drainage, wheat, vegetables, fruit and flowers are grown in the fertile fields. But in the Middle Ages, Norfolk was a water-ridden fen used only by hunters, fishermen and solitary shepherds. In the north lies the Wash — a wide shallow bay between the counties of Norfolk and Lincolnshire. There were few towns in the Middle Ages, none of them on the coastline of the Wash. The ancient port of King's Lynn lay upstream on the River Ouse. A deep sound through the Wash made it accessible to sea-going vessels. It's still a busy port today.

The main export from King's Lynn in the Middle Ages was wool. And the main imports were the foreign pilgrims, on their way to the Shrine of our Lady at nearby Walsingham. It was the most important holy place in Mediaeval England, and the trade made King's Lynn prosperous. The fine Mediaeval church of St Margaret's, with its unusual twin towers, was built at this time of prosperity. And the names of many of the streets — Greyfriars, Whitefriars and Blackfriars — remind the visitor that there were many monasteries at King's Lynn. This was a typical Mediaeval English country town and port, yet with a strong continental influence because of the visits of the pilgrims. They came, in particular, from Germany and the Low Countries.

At the turn of the fifteenth century, Margery Kempe attended St Margaret's Church. She could, perhaps, be called a saint. She was born in 1373, and her father was the Mayor. Most of us think of saints as people who have cut themselves off from ordinary life. But the market place was Margery's natural environment — that and the church. Margery was an ordinary parishioner, taught by the priests. She attended the fasts and the festivals of the Church. Often she was involved in parish squabbles. But she never read the Bible for herself — because she could not read. Nor did she understand Latin, the language of the Bible in her time.

Even the ordinary clergy of Margery's day were relatively uneducated. They knew best the epistles and the gospels which were read at the Mass. Margery was taught what the priests of the Church were able to teach her. But there are many different ways of understanding religion, emotional as well as intellectual. The mind leads to study, to scholarship and to discussion, but the feelings are more likely to lead to prayer.

Margery may have been unlettered, but she certainly prayed. She had remarkable, dream-like visions in her prayers. Towards the end of her life, she dictated her religious experiences so that they could be written down. The result was *The Book of Margery Kempe*. In her visions she relived the stories of Jesus in the New Testament. In her prayers, the crucifixion at Calvary came alive as though she was actually there, and everything was happening in the present. In this scene from her book, a priest has found her in a church. She is weeping as she looks at a crucifix. It brings it all back to her — but she annoys the priest:

MALE READER
        Don't cry lady, he died a long time ago.
        He pauses
        He died a very long time ago!
FEMALE READER
        His death is as fresh to me as if he had died this same day . . . and
        so I think it ought to be to you and to all Christian people.

Margery was certainly a disturbing parishioner. She relived the crucifixion time and time again, and it often brought her to tears. To her, it was no historic event but a vital and painful truth in the present. In her prayers, she spoke to Jesus, to the Virgin Mary and to the saints. But Margery was thoroughly English. The world of the Holy Land in the first century was somehow tranformed in her prayers to the context of fourteenth century King's Lynn with its busy port and visiting pilgrims. Unlike study, prayer is a matter of here and now.

QUESTIONS FOR DEBATE

1. Do you think Margery would have understood her religion better if she had been able to read and write?
2. Why is prayer a matter of here and now?

November the fifth   (4 mins)

Catherine wheels and rockets, Roman candles and bangers — that's November the fifth. It's eating hot dogs around bonfires, the smoke swirling, the people in heavy coats laughing and joking. It's children running around, playing silly tricks on each other and making circles in the night air with their sparklers. And why do we have this winter festival? Because, on November the fifth in 1605, a gang of conspirators tried to blow up Parliament.

The story really starts a lot earlier. The kings and queens of England in the fifteenth century had far greater personal power than any other monarchs before or since. When Henry VIII came to the throne in 1509, he seemed the best King of England for centuries. He was a fine athlete, a musician, a theologian. There seemed nothing that he could not do . . . except that his wife, a Spanish princess called Catherine, could not give him a son. The story is well known. In 1533, after Henry had been refused a divorce by the Pope, he took Anne Boleyn as his second wife and separated the Church of England from the Roman Catholic Church. In this, he was supported by Thomas Cranmer, Archbishop of Canterbury. Henry was declared head of the Church 'in this realm of England'. It was the beginning of a long and bitter struggle.

Henry was followed by his son, Edward VI. During his short reign, the Book of Common Prayer appeared and services in the churches were in English for the first time. Thomas Cranmer was responsible for producing the Prayer Book.

Let's imagine the scene at the University Church of St Mary the Virgin in Oxford on 21st March, 1556. By that time, Queen Mary was on the throne. She was the daughter of Henry's first wife, Catherine, and was intent on returning England into the fold of the Roman Catholic Church. The University Church was crowded to hear a sermon. In front of the pulpit, on a low scaffold, was Archbishop Cranmer. Dr Coles, the preacher, said that Cranmer had admitted that he was wrong. Then he went on to explain why the prisoner was nevertheless to be burnt at the stake. He had divorced the Queen's mother. He had drawn a blemish on her birth, and he had thrown the Pope's supremacy out of the kingdom. It is reported that the Archbishop wept during the sermon. When it was over, Cranmer was taken into the centre of Broad Street in Oxford and burnt to death.

This is only one example. Those Tudor kings and queens used execution as an instrument of policy. The list of great men who died at their command reads like a 'Who's Who' of sixteenth century churchmen. On June 27th, 1581, there was yet another scene at the same church. By that time Elizabeth I was Queen. She wanted a Church of England independent of Rome. But at the University Church of St Mary the Virgin was a man who disagreed. His name was Edmund Campion. During the service he distributed to the congregation four hundred copies of a leaflet in favour of a return to the Roman Catholic Church. It was a public act

. . . and suicidal. Campion was taken to the Tower of London and hanged.

There were martyrs on both sides, and strong feelings on both sides. And those Tudor kings and queens wrenched the Church first one way, then the other. The idea of destroying both the king and the parliament at one fell swoop came during the reign of James I. Robert Catesby, Thomas Winter, Thomas Percy, John Wright and Guy Fawkes were the conspirators who placed the twenty or so kegs of gunpowder in the cellar. Had they succeeded, England would have been without government. They hoped that, in the confusion that would follow, English Roman Catholics could take over the country.

These days, in most of the towns and villages of this country, there are Councils of Churches. Christians of all denominations take part — Anglicans, Roman Catholics, Methodists and many others. The differences in outlook between them are still real enough, but the bitter quarrels of the past are gone. Perhaps Councils of Churches would be the best people to run firework parties on Bonfire Night. It would be a sign that the old hatreds are going up in flames.

QUESTIONS FOR DEBATE

1. What does Cranmer's execution tell us about the monarchy of the time?
2. Was Cranmer wrong to claim that he had changed his mind?

The Great Plague   (7 mins)

Daniel Defoe wrote novels. But he lived at a time when Puritanism was very strong in England. The Puritans claimed that, since novels were fiction, they should be classed as lies and should therefore not be tolerated. They had succeeded in closing down many of the theatres in London for the same reason. To avoid coming into conflict with the Puritans, Defoe decided to present his novels as fact rather than fiction. And the stories he wrote were, indeed, based on fact. His most famous novel, *Robinson Crusoe,* was based on the story of Alexander Selkirk, a man who had been marooned on the island of Juan Fernandez for four years.

In 1722, he published a book entitled *A Journal of the Plague Year*. He claimed that it had been written by a man who had lived in London during the Great Plague.

Almost certainly, that was not true. But Defoe's method of basing his writings on facts means that this book is likely to be a reliable historical account of the plague. Defoe himself was only five years old at the time of the Great Plague, but when he wrote *A Journal of the Plague Year* fifty-seven years later, he knew that there were people still living who remembered it better than he did. He could not afford to make mistakes.

In Defoe's book, we see the great city of London virtually closed down from July 1665 to the end of the following year. He tells the story of a group of people who tried to escape from the city where the plague raged at its worst. They wanted to go into the country:

READER
> When they came to Walthamstow, the people of the time denied to admit them, as was the case everywhere. The constables and their watchmen kept them off at a distance and parleyed with them.

They refused even to let the strangers pass through the town, for fear that they were plague carriers. The travellers, under their leader John, were obliged to trick the townspeople:

> He set the joiner, Richard, to work to cut down some poles out of the trees and shape them as like guns as he could, and in a little time he had five or six fair muskets, which at a distance could not be known . . .

Setting up a tent in full view of the town, John placed a sentry before it, and tethered their only horse nearby:

> . . . perceiving they had horses and arms, for they had seen one horse and one gun at the tent . . . they were alarmed and terribly frightened.

By this trick, the travellers not only gained access through Walthamstow, but provisions as well from the frightened townspeople.

It was the overwhelming fear of the plague which forced people to take such desperate measures. The laws, made in an attempt to contain the plague, were very harsh. The constables and wardens enforced these laws. Infected people, together with their whole families, were locked up in their houses, leading very often to more deaths than was necessary. The gathering of people in large groups was, so far as possible, prohibited by law:

READER

...all plays, bear-baitings, games, singing of ballads, buckler-play or such-like causes of assemblies of people utterly prohibited.

And any kind of public feasting, including 'dinners at taverns, ale-houses and other places of common entertainment', was stopped, and nobody was allowed to enter an alehouse after nine in the evening.

The plague was, in fact, passed on by rat fleas, and many of the regulations did nothing to stop its progress. It was lack of knowledge, rather than anything else, which caused so much human suffering. It was a common belief, shared by Defoe, that the plague was God's punishment for the wickedness of the people. Defoe's father saw it as a reward for his own righteousness. As many people were put out of business, it gave him the opportunity to become a successful butcher.

No disease on the same scale as the plague has happened in England since. No doubt, if it did, people would react in much the same way, defending their own lives and homes, shunning strangers and travellers.

QUESTIONS FOR DEBATE

1. Do you think the Puritans were in any way right in condemning novels and plays as 'lies'?
2. Do you think that it is right for people to want to defend themselves when public disaster occurs?

The Great Fire   (5 mins)

Samuel Pepys was a civil servant in the Admiralty during one of the most turbulent periods in English history. The Civil War between the Roundheads and the Cavaliers raged during his childhood. Then came the execution of Charles I, and the period of the Commonwealth under Oliver Cromwell. With the Restoration, Charles II came to the throne and, soon after, there was the Great Plague and the Fire of London. The historians are very grateful to Samuel Pepys. He decided to keep a detailed diary of his life in London during much of this period. Yet the diary is much more than a piece of useful history. It is a day to day eyewitness account of events, a lively piece of literature. Pepys often tells of small everyday events with as much enthusiasm as when he is describing happenings which have changed the course of history:

READER

> Sept. 1, 1666 . . . Sir W. Penn and my wife and Mercer and I to 'Polichanelly', but were there horribly frightened to see young Kilgrew come in with a great many more young sparks; but we hid ourselves, so as we think they did not see us. By and by they went away, and then we were at rest again; but the play being done, we to Islington and there to eat and drink and mighty merry – and so home, singing; and after a letter or two at the office, to bed.

Henry Kilgrew, like Pepys, worked for the Duke of York. Pepys was not at all keen that his employer should know that he had been out on the town the night before, and Kilgrew might have mentioned it. Pepys, after all, held a very responsible position.

The following day, though, records a very much more important event:

READER

> Sept. 2, 1666 . . . Some of our maids sitting up last night to get things ready against our feast today, Jane called us up about 3 in the morning, to tell us a great fire they saw in the City. So I rose and slipped on my nightgown and went to her window, and thought it to be on the back side of Markelane at the furthest; but being unused to such fires, I thought it far enough off, and so went to bed again, and to sleep. About 7 rose again to dress myself, and there looked out at the window and saw the fire not so much as it was, and further off. So to my closet to set things to right after yesterday's cleaning. By and by Jane comes and tells me she hears above 300 houses have been burned down tonight by the fire we saw, and that it was now burning down all Fish Street by London Bridge . . .

The fire, which had been started accidentally at about two in the morning in a bakery in Pudding Lane was to burn for four days and nights, destroying four fifths of the old city of London including about thirteen thousand, two hundred houses.

That day, Pepys travelled by boat down the Thames in order to get as close as he could to the fire. He was horrified by what he saw, as people desperately tried to save their possessions — even, as a last resort, throwing them in the river. Worse, he saw the wind driving the flames towards the city, 'and everything, after so long a drought, proving combustible, even the very stones of the churches'. Pepys then went to see his employer, the Duke of York, who was in conference with King Charles II. He urged them that the only way to stop the fire was to pull down the houses in the path of the flames, and so contain it. The king agreed, and Pepys was told to order the Lord Mayor of London to do it:

READER

> At last met my Lord Mayor in Canning Street, like a man spent, with a handkercher about his neck. To the king's message, he cried like a fainting woman, 'Lord, what can I do? I am spent. People will not obey me. I have been pulling down houses. But the fire overtakes us much faster than we can do it.'

There was nothing to stop the fire in the meandering narrow streets of wood-framed houses and the strong east wind swept it onwards, the disaster going from bad to worse. On the evening of the 2nd September, Pepys watched the city he had known all his life going up in smoke. The diary betrays his feelings very well:

READER

> We to a little alehouse on the Bankside over against the Three Cranes, and stayed there till it was dark almost and saw the fire grow; and as it grew darker, appeared more and more, and in corners and upon steeples and between churches and houses, so far as we could see up the hill of the City, a most horrid, malicious, bloody flame, not like the fine flame of an ordinary fire . . . We stayed till, it being darkish, we saw the fire as only one entire arch of flame from this to the other side of the bridge, and in a bow up the hill, for an arch above a mile long. It made me weep to see it.

It became clear that Pepys' own house was now in immediate danger. He rushed home to pack his things. The packing went on all night, and his most valuable possessions were sent to the house of a friend at Bethnal Green, well out of the range of the flames. Having barely eaten or slept since that first day of the fire, on the fifth Pepys and his family heard the cries of 'Fire!' close to their home.

It had reached the bottom of their lane. Pepys lost no time in taking members of his household down river to Woolwich, before he returned once more to see what could be done. He arrived at his road, fully expecting to see his house ablaze, but, to his surprise, houses in the path of the flames had been blown up creating a form of fire ditch. More importantly, the wind had changed and the worst of the fire was over. Pepys' house had been saved, but the main part of the city had been destroyed. Among the buildings burnt down was the great Mediaeval Cathedral of St Paul's in the heart of the city.

QUESTIONS FOR DEBATE

1. Everybody has heard of the Great Fire of London, but why does a personal diary bring the tragedy to life?
2. Two factors made the Great Fire possible – a long drought and a strong east wind. Very often, disasters are caused by the forces of nature. Does that make if difficult to believe in a God who cares for people?

H.M.S. Victory   (4 mins)

In 1559, a warship of 800 tons called H.M.S. Victory was added to the Elizabethan navy. The ship had an illustrious career and was the flagship of Sir John Hawkins, third in command of the British fleet at the defeat of the Spanish Armada in 1588. So began a famous name in the history of the navy. In the following hundred and fifty years, no fewer than three other warships were named 'Victory' at various points.

The fifth H.M.S. Victory is still berthed in Number 2 Dock at Portsmouth Harbour. She was begun in 1758 at Chatham on the Medway, part of a programme of building twelve ships of the line. This was the period of the Seven Years' War, a struggle between the European powers. Britain was allied with Prussia against France, Russia and Austria. Usually such a ship took five years to build, but the British military successes, which led to control both of India and of North America, lessened the sense of urgency. H.M.S. Victory was indeed built at a time of victory for the British. She was not launched until 1765 and, for thirteen years, she remained in her home port.

The Victory became flagship to a series of admirals. In 1794, she was the flagship of Admiral Lord Hood when he was involved in operations in Corsica against the forces of revolutionary France. Guns and men were landed from the Victory to siege Calvi, under the command of Captain Horatio Nelson. It was the beginning of the association of the famous man and the famous ship. In that engagement, a French bullet threw up debris which destroyed Nelson's right eye.

The following year, the Victory became flagship to Admiral Sir John Jervis. Squadrons of Spanish, French and Dutch ships were gathering at Cape St Vincent for an invasion of Britain. The Spanish were sailing in two divisions through the mist. The British admiral planned to cut between them and to attack one before the other could come up. But he miscalculated, and passed between them. By the time his ships had turned, it would be too late. Without orders from Jervis, Nelson threw his ship, the Captain, into the path of the closing columns of vessels. He held the two Spanish squadrons apart, at one time engaging seven ships all at once. The accuracy of the British gunnery won the day. Nelson took one enemy ship, and used it to board another. Jervis was awarded the earldom of St Vincent as a result of this battle, and Nelson was made a knight.

In the years that followed, Nelson won a series of famous victories. But the ship which is most associated with his name was not involved. In 1797, the Victory returned to Chatham and was paid off. Between 1798 and 1800 she was used as a hospital ship for the prison hulks. Then, in 1801, she underwent an extensive refit. She was recommissioned in April 1803 and, in July, she arrived in the Mediterranean as flagship of Lord Nelson, Commander-in-Chief.

On 15th September, 1805, H.M.S. Victory left England to take over the command of the fleet blockading Cadiz. In this way the scene was set for one of the most decisive battles ever fought at sea. On 21st October, off Cape Trafalgar, the British fleet vanquished the combined fleets of France and Spain. Of the thirty-three enemy ships, eighteen were taken; four escaped only to be rounded up a fortnight later; the remainder struggled back into Cadiz to remain there for the rest of the war against Napoleon. The French were finally denied mastery of the sea. Yet for the British, this was not so much a day of victory as one of profound sorrow. At about 1.25 p.m., towards the end of the engagement, Nelson was walking in the quarter deck with Captain Hardy. A shot from the mizzen top of the French ship Redoutable, about forty feet away, went through Nelson's backbone. The hero of Trafalgar was taken below and died in the cockpit of the ship shortly after.

No British national hero has ever been mourned as Nelson was mourned. In the spit and sawdust dockside taverns of London, strong men wept. He was loved as much there as in the royal court or the great country houses of England. His audacity made him the idol of every small boy in the land. His death was treated as a national disaster. On the day of Trafalgar before the battle, Nelson sat in his day cabin composing a prayer:

READER

> May the great God whom I worship grant to my Country, and for the benefit of Europe in general, a great and glorious victory; and may no misconduct in any one tarnish it; and may humanity after victory be the predominant feature in the British fleet. For myself individually I commit my life to Him that made me, and may His blessing light upon my endeavours for serving my Country faithfully. To Him I resign myself and the just cause which is entrusted to me to defend.

QUESTIONS FOR DEBATE

1. Why do you think so many people thought of Nelson as a hero?
2. What does the prayer tell you about his state of mind on the day of the battle?

Allen Gardiner   (6 mins)

When Admiral Lord Nelson died at Cape Trafalgar off the coast of Spain in 1805, a profound surge of emotion gripped the whole country. Even the hardened dockers in the spit and sawdust bars of the East End of London wept. The great national hero was killed in the midst of an outstanding victory. It gave Britain the mastery of the seas. Nelson's flagship, H.M.S. Victory, is still docked in the harbour at Portsmouth in his honour.

Upstream from Reading, in the country house called Coombe Lodge, standing above water-meadows that border the Thames on the outskirts of the village of Whitchurch, there lived a boy of ten. His name was Allen Gardiner, the fifth son of the family. Like a multitude of boys of the time, he had no thought in his mind except Nelson and the sea. In 1808, he entered the Naval College at Portsmouth, and his career had begun. At sixteen, he was a midshipman on H.M.S. Fortune, a man-of-war of the Royal Navy.

Allen Gardiner was a born adventurer. If he entered a foreign port, he went by himself on long sightseeing expeditions and made contact with the native people. He first saw action at sea against the Americans. In the war between Britain and France, America had begun to grow rich by selling supplies to both sides. But after Trafalgar, Britain demanded that this trade should cease. American ships were seized for ignoring the order. Allen Gardiner was one of the British sailors to board an American ship called the 'Essex' in the Pacific in 1815. The 'Essex' had been heavily bombarded, and a scene of carnage greeted his eyes. He was one of the sailors detailed to bring the captured ship back to Portsmouth.

At Portsmouth, Allen Gardiner bought a Bible. No doubt, the reasons for it were many and complex. He had been brought up in a Christian home. And he had become acutely aware of the cheapness of human life during his time at sea. His next voyage was to Penang in China. He often spoke later of a profound spiritual experience during a visit to one of the temples at Penang. So began Allen Gardiner's lifelong attachment to religion and the Christian faith.

In 1821, Gardiner was serving on H.M.S. Dauntless on a voyage to the ports of Chile and Peru. As he understood it, the Spanish and Portuguese colonists had done great damage to these countries. And, with his English Protestant background, he particularly disliked the influence wielded by the Roman Catholic Church. Only the native tribes who had first inhabited these countries were not affected. They kept far from the cities, and continued their traditional nomadic manner of life. Gardiner developed a great admiration for them.

That voyage on the Dauntless was a turning point in Gardiner's life. The ship stopped at Tahiti on the way back. He was astonished to notice that, unlike other places, the natives did not swarm in their canoes around the ship, bartering the local wares. Instead, everybody had gone to church because it was Sunday. Tahiti was unique at that time. Both the king and the population of the island had become fervent Christians. From then on, it was Gardiner's dream to bring the same sort of faith to other native peoples.

His first act on arriving home was to approach the London Missionary Society to seek support for a mission to the natives of South America. The idea was turned down. The Society simply did not have the funds. Gardiner then approached the Bishop of Gloucester, seeking to become a clergyman of the Church of England. That too was refused. So Gardiner stayed in the Navy. He settled down and got married. His home was 'Swanmore House', near Droxford in Hampshire. Little is known of him at that time. Two of his five children died in infancy and, in 1834, his wife also died. This was the signal for Gardiner to go into action.

His first missionary venture was not to South America, but to the Zulus of South Africa. At that time, the Zulus' reputation for cruelty was such that his friends were convinced they would never see him again. When Gardiner arrived at Port Natal, he discovered that Dingaan, the Zulu chieftain, was the greatest threat to peace. Dingaan had extended his Zulu empire by ruthlessly destroying hundreds of African villages and slaughtering their inhabitants.

Gardiner made a solitary trek, accompanied by native guides and an interpreter, to see Dingaan. The chief received him quite cordially. It took time, but in the end Gardiner gained his confidence. On his second visit, he took Dingaan a great many gifts. The most exciting, so far as the Zulu chieftain was concerned, was a telescope. In return, Dingaan gave him 'the whole territory beyond the mountains right to the sea', as his personal possession. But Gardiner convinced Dingaan that the land should be given instead, one king to another, to King William IV. The idea pleased Dingaan. And, more important so far as Gardiner was concerned, he was given permission to send a missionary to the native peoples.

Did the mission succeed? No. Within a short time, a series of local battles had broken out. South Africa was a volatile mixture of natives, British and Dutch, all laying claim to territory. Gardiner returned to England. In the years that followed, he made missionary journeys to the natives of many of the South American countries. Each time, he tried to stay with the local people, to learn their language and to tell them about the Bible. Always the mission came to nothing.

But Gardiner was certainly persistent. In the end, he and four companions went on a mission to the natives of Tierra del Fuego — an archipelago of islands at the very extremity of South America. Because the natives stole everything in sight, they kept their belongings on board two large boats which they had brought with them. But hostile natives drove them from one place to another, and soon one of their boats was crippled in a remote cove where no ship was likely to find them. To add to their troubles, months of living on a poor diet was affecting their health. One by one they died. Gardiner was the last. He died on 6th September, 1851. The bodies of the five men were discovered about four months later.

It might seem that Allen Gardiner's life was a complete failure. A leading article in the Times newspaper on 24th April, 1852 thundered about the waste of lives and money 'on hoardes of savages at the other side of the world'. The reaction to it was to arouse a new enthusiasm for the work which Gardiner had attempted to begin. Today, the South American Missionary Society, inspired by Gardiner, continues to work in the towns and cities of many of the countries where the efforts of the man himself came to nothing. And, these days, the Society co-operates with the clergy of the Roman Catholic Church.

QUESTIONS FOR DEBATE

1. Why did Gardiner so admire Tahiti?
2. Suggest reasons why Gardiner disliked the Roman Catholic Church.

A young parson visits the Hughes family   (6 mins)

In 1937, a magazine called 'Farmer's Weekly' serialized a diary which had been kept, so the readers were told, by a Mrs Anne Hughes during the early years of the nineteenth century. She was, according to the diary, a farmer's wife on a remote Herefordshire farm. But after a while, people began to ask questions. Where exactly did Anne Hughes live? Could her name be found in other records? What evidence was there, apart from the diary printed in the magazine, that she had ever existed? As time went by, suspicions grew that the whole story had been a forgery created by Jeanne Preston, the farm manager's wife who had supplied it to the magazine. Soon it was described as 'that old fraud'.

Nowadays, people are not so sure that the diary was a forgery. Jeanne Preston is now dead, but her daughter Molly says that she remembers the diary itself; a thin book full of spidery writing. But whether the diary is genuine or not, one thing is certain. It describes life on a remote hill farm in Herefordshire soon after 1800 very well. Let's see what it says about country life at that time.

One of the centres of village life in Anne Hughes' time was the church. The village parson was an important member of the community, and churchgoing on a Sunday brought people together. The parson, too, visited the farms and was often entertained to a meal. His visiting usually involved long rides on horseback, and the country people were very hospitable. It's interesting to read what Anne Hughes' diary tells us about the coming of a new parson to her village. Remember that she wrote in the Herefordshire accent of the time:

READER
>   Sept. ye 9 — John cums in to say he will let the cider makeing stop
>   till Tewesday, now that passon be cumming. I be verrie glad to hear
>   this. Bein bussie I cannot write more in my book but we to bed.

John was Anne Hughes' husband and, at that time of the year, they were both much involved in the making of rough Herefordshire cider. But the promise of a visit by the new parson was enough to put a stop to the work. Let's continue:

READER
>   Sept. ye 13 — The new passon cum on Saterday; a yound lad of 20
>   yeres or so. I be glad we did so much cookeing for he did ett much,
>   being clemmed of his journie. We to church on the Sabboth, and did
>   heare a plessent sermon. John did nod as alwayes, but the passon did

pleese me much, for he did not tell us that the divvel would hav us for caring for sum monies, but did say the world be a verrie good plase to live in; and be good to the poore, was the true religun, to which I do hartilie agree.

You can see that the ideas about religion in the diary are very simple. Anne Hughes did not want to be made to feel guilty because she and her husband had money. She enjoyed her life, but she did believe that it was important to give to the poor and was glad to be reminded of it by the parson. An important part of Sunday in those days was the Sunday dinner:

READER

Then we home to dinner, carrying off Mistress Prue ande her sister Livvie; where we did find Sarah had put all reddie. We did have roste goose stuffed with boiled egges and sweete appels, which did cum out nice and jouisey; sum shepe mutton, and 2 roste hens; and round of befe boiled, and taties and soe on — as well as mylke pudden, and a appel and divers others. To which all did do justis, and Mistress Prue praising Sarahs cookeing much, did pleese me. And I did see passon look at Sarah verrie prettie.

You can see why Anne Hughes did not believe in being poor. She and her guests had plenty to eat at their Sunday dinner. And she liked her parsons to be human. She noticed the glances of admiration which the young parson sent in the direction of Sarah, the maid.

It doesn't seem to matter whether the diary of Anne Hughes is a forgery or not. It describes very well the attitude of people who were very close to the land, and who found it natural to believe in a God who made the land fertile.

QUESTIONS FOR DEBATE

1. Before publishing the work, should the 'Farmer's Weekly' have made certain that Anne Hughes' diary was not a forgery?
2. There were many poor people in England in the period when Anne Hughes was supposed to have lived. Do you think the diary makes her appear selfish?

One of Tom Hood's puzzles   (4 mins)

Thomas Hood was born in London in 1799, the son of a publisher and bookseller. As a boy, he was trained as an engraver, but he soon discovered that he had a talent for writing poetry. It was not a good time for poets. People did not want to buy books of serious poetry. But Hood found that, if he wrote comic poems, people would buy them. Hood's sense of humour seems to us very strange. He saw the funny side of terrible events. A funeral, for instance, was always good for a laugh. And if wild animals were about to tear each other apart, there was a joke in it for Hood. Let's read such a poem and see what he makes of it. It's called 'The language of hunger intelligible'. When the poem speaks of pigs, it's important to think of wild boars — ferocious and dangerous animals:

READER
          Said the young pig to the old pig,
            'Umph, umph, umph, umph!'
          Said the old pig to the young pig,
            'Grumph, grumph, grumph, grumph!'
          But what was their meaning I cannot disclose,
            Since the language of piggiwigs nobody knows.

You notice the way Hood has made the grunting of the old pig gruffer than the grunting of the young pig. It's the difference between 'umph' and 'grumph'. This kind of poetry owes a great deal, of course, to nursery rhymes. The word 'pig-giwig', for instance, is a nursery word. Very small children use it, but it sounds funny when said by adults. Let's move on:

READER
          Said the young pig to the old pig,
            'Squeak, squeak, squeak, squeak!'
          Said the old pig to the young pig,
            'Week, week, week, week!'
          But what they intended surpasses my knowledge;
            The tongue is a tongue they don't teach in college.

You notice that Hood's young pig is far better at squealing than the old pig. And he makes a joke of the idea that people who have been to college are supposed to know a lot. Yet no human being knows what pigs say to each other. Things get a bit nasty in the next verse:

READER

> Said the thin wolf to the fat pig –
>   Never a word.
> What the fat pig to the thin wolf
>   Replied, I've not heard.
> But though unacquainted with either's remark,
> As touching their meanings I'm not in the dark.

Many people see nature as showing God's goodness. But Hood shows the other side of the coin. Nature can be violent, 'red in tooth and claw'. We may not know what animals mean when they make their noises, but we know exactly what they mean when they are starving or when they are threatened. Hood included with his poem a translation of the unspoken conversation between the wolf and the wild boar:

READER

> 'My appetite,' wolf says, 'needs nothing to whet it:
> I doat upon pork, though it's long since I ate it!'
> 'Indeed!' says the boar, 'don't you wish you may get it?'

Hood called his poem 'The language of hunger intelligible', of course, because it amused him to be able to include a translation of the unspoken conversation. But the point which is being made is serious enough – and it doesn't just apply to the animal kingdom. So often, people too have caused trouble because while one man starves, another has plenty.

QUESTIONS FOR DEBATE

1. Many people these days are vegetarians. Do you think it is wrong for us to eat the flesh of other animals?
2. What examples have you seen of intelligence in animals?

Death of an old mendicant   (4 mins)

William McGonagall was a handloom weaver in Dundee. He was born in Glasgow
in 1830. In his spare time, however, he also acted and wrote poetry. Nobody knows
what his acting was like, but his poetry was special — he was easily the worst
poet to write in English. It is virtually impossible to get down to his level. The
truth of the matter is that the poetry which he took very seriously indeed makes
people laugh. As a result, his works are still selling in the bookshops today. Let's
look at one of his poems. It's called 'The death of the poor mendicant'. The word
'mendicant' simply means 'beggar'. (The poetry is best declaimed, if possible, with
a Scottish accent.)

READER

There was a rich old gentleman
Lived on a lonely moor in Switzerland,
And he was very hard to the wandering poor,
'Tis said he never lodged nor served them at his door.

'Twas on a stormy night, and Boreas blew a bitter blast,
And the snowflakes they fell thick and fast
When a poor old mendicant, tired and footsore,
Who had travelled that day fifteen miles and more,
Knocked loudly at the rich man's door.

It's the tone of the poetry, I suppose, that people find funny. You imagine his craggy
Scottish face, hell-bent on drumming home his message and quite unwilling to
leave the slightest thought out, however obvious. After all, if the old mendicant
was described as 'tired and footsore', there was no real need to say that he had
travelled 'fifteen mile and more'. But McGonagall was quite sure his readers were
idiots, so he put it in. Let's read some more:

READER

The rich man was in his parlour counting his gold,
And he ran to the door to see who was so bold,
And there he saw the mendicant shivering with the cold.

Then the mendicant said unto him,
My dear sir, be not afraid,
Pray give me lodgings for the night,
And heaven will your love requite;
Have pity on me, for I am tired and footsore,
I have travelled today fifteen miles and more.

Begone! you vagabond, from my door!
I never give lodgings to the poor;
So be off, take to your heels and run,
Or else I'll shoot you with my gun
Now do not think I'm making fun;
Do you hear, old beggar, what I say?

Now be quick! and go away.

You would have thought that McGonagall would have left it there, but the poem continues to emphasise the obvious:

READER
Have mercy, sir, I cannot go,
For I shall perish in the snow,
Oh! for heaven's sake, be not so hard,
And God will your love reward,
My limbs are tired, I cannot go away,
Oh! be so kind as to let me stay.
'Twas vain! the rich man said, I shan't
And shut his door on the mendicant,
And said, That is the way I'll serve the poor
While I live on this lonely moor.

If you wanted to teach people how to write, perhaps a good method would be to show them how McGonagall wrote and then tell them to do the opposite. His writing breaks practically every rule. He doesn't describe his characters. All he tells us about the rich man is that he is 'counting his gold'. What else would a rich man do? Nor do we get any picture of the mendicant, except that he is a beggar and that he's likely to go on about it – at least McGonagall goes on about it. McGonagall repeats himself over and over again. Perhaps the most important rule in writing is never to do the obvious. McGonagall makes a speciality of always doing the obvious. Long before another master of obvious writing – the author of the *Rupert Bear* books — had burst on the scene, McGonagall had shown the way. Which do you think is worse?

> And Rupert sat down at the table,
> And ate as much has he was able.

or

> Have mercy, sir, I cannot go,
> For I shall perish in the snow.

Having read that much of the poem, I'm sure you can guess what happens at the end. It can be told in one sentence, but McGonagall takes another twenty-three lines to say it. The old mendicant dies in the snow and the rich man is so ashamed that he changes his ways.

We could easily go on, of course, making fun of McGonagall and his little moral tales. But I think it's also important to take him seriously. He may have made a speciality of bad poetry, but it is also clear that he was an honest and sincere man with a firm belief in God and a real desire to teach people to give to the poor. In Victorian times, there was a much greater contrast between the rich and the poor than there is today. Many of the writers of the time showed how the poor lived and helped to change attitudes. Yet even today, there are people sleeping rough on park benches in our cities. The problem has not disappeared.

QUESTIONS FOR DEBATE

1. Do you think McGonagall's poetry is worth reading?
2. How do you think more can be done to help poor people today?

Mayflower II   (5 mins)

In the reign of Elizabeth I, people were expected to belong to the Church of England, and laws were passed to punish people who wanted to worship in other ways. Roman Catholic priests said the Mass in secret, and those who were caught were usually hanged or burnt at the stake. But the Elizabethan authorities were just as severe with the Protestants. The idea of a 'Congregational' church came into being at about this time — a church in which all members played an equal part. Some of the Congregationalists were also executed for their beliefs. Nor were matters very different under James I in the following reign. For some people, the only answer was to leave England. Many English Congregationalists settled in Holland. But the most famous of all these emigrations was to America. The Pilgrim Fathers, as they have been called, set sail from the port of Southampton in a ship called the Mayflower on August 17th, 1620.

In 1957 at the shipyard of Brixham in Devon, shipwrights started to build a replica of the Mayflower. This was to be Mayflower II, and the intention was to relive the experiences of those Pilgrim Fathers of three hundred and thirty-seven years earlier. Many people said it could not be done. Such a vessel had not been built since the seventeenth century. And it seemed unlikely that the seamanship required to sail her would be available in an age when modern ships required quite different skills.

The craftsmen who built Mayflower II decided to be faithful to the techniques in use when the first Mayflower was built. They used only the tools which had been available for the building of the original ship. The woods of Devon were scoured for oak trees which could supply the planks. Blacksmiths with furnaces, anvils and hammers shaped the ironwork for the rigging and the rudder. Gradually, the little ship began to take shape. She was small, sound and well-built, just over a hundred and six feet long. A Scottish firm searched the company records of two hundred years earlier to find out how the rigging was to be made. When the keel was launched, Mayflower II immediately fell over on her side. Such a ship needed ballast, and that could not be loaded in the shallow water of the modern dock. 'Mayflower capsizes!', shouted the newspaper headlines. But once the ship was weighted down with railway iron, she rode easily in the water.

At last Mayflower II set sail into the English Channel on an April morning. Her crew wore the same sort of clothing as had been worn by the crewmen of the original Mayflower. No modern equipment, apart from navigational instruments, had been included. At night there were guttering candles instead of steady electric lights. Sailing her in rough water, it turned out, was alarming. She could buck and swerve wildly, and even the most experienced sailors among the crew were seasick. The masts whipped around describing great circles against the sky. Climbing the rigging under such conditions was frightening. Captain Alan Villiers decided to sail south, seeking good weather, rather than make his way directly across the Atlantic where there were likely to be rough passages.

The southern route, utilizing the trade winds, took Mayflower II down the west coast of France and Spain. At first, she made up to a hundred and fifty miles in a day. The sun shone and Felix, the ship's cat, curled up on the warm deck. Felix was a regular member of the crew. With a lifejacket made by one of the seamen, the cat was expected to join in the regular lifeboat drills. After the Canary Islands, Mayflower II headed west. Now the winds dropped, and the little ship had difficulty in making five hundred miles in a week. One day the captain actually logged twenty miles backwards! At this point in the voyage, progress was slow in the extreme. This was the route which had been sailed by Christopher Columbus to discover the New World. He had a flotilla of small ships not very different from Mayflower II. The occasional threat of an electric storm on the edge of the tropics reminded the crewmen of the fears felt by Columbus and his sailors when this route was followed for the first time in history.

As Mayflower II approached the West Indies, the winds freshened. She bowled along in full sail, the waters curling beneath her bow. Nothing like her had been seen for centuries, and passing shipping made a point of saluting the little vessel. She was a picture straight out of a romantic history book of the sea. The voyage was coming, so it seemed, to a triumphant and graceful end. But there was one more test.

Suddenly and unexpectedly, a wild gale blew up. As the winds blew harder and the seas grew more mountainous, the mariners took in the sails one by one. This was becoming the supreme test of the seaworthiness of Mayflower II. The square-rigged spritsail in the bow caused the greatest problems. Four sailors went out on the shuddering bowsprit and along the yard to bring in canvas thrashing and thundering in the wild wind. If a man had fallen off, there was no way of rescuing him from the sea below. They mastered the spritsail. Then the ship's company swarmed aloft to furl the last of the sails. It was then that Captain Villiers discovered one of the secrets of life at sea in the seventeenth century. Once the canvas was off, he could hold her shoulder to the sea and Mayflower II rode out the storm safely and quietly. 'I was never so quiet in a ship in a gale of wind at sea before, nor felt so safe', said Godfrey Wicksteed, the ship's mate.

When Captain Christopher Jones had sailed with the Pilgrim Fathers in the first Mayflower, there were about a hundred and thirty people aboard, and the voyage took sixty-seven days. It took Mayflower II, only fifty-four days to reach her mooring at Plymouth, Massachusetts. She was greeted with great excitement in the United States. Thirty-one men, two boys and one cat had made the voyage. Modern regulations forbad the crowded conditions of the first Mayflower. The intention of the people who made possible the voyage of Mayflower II was to relive the voyage of the Mayflower. But there was a further, quite different purpose. Mayflower II had aboard an exhibition of British goods, with the intention of promoting trade with the United States.

QUESTIONS FOR DEBATE

1. There were five thousand volunteers who wished to become crew members on Mayflower II. Why did so many people want to make the voyage?
2. Why were the sailors, during part of this voyage, haunted by thoughts of Christopher Columbus?

No Heaven for Gunga Din   (6 mins)

In 1943, when British and American forces had invaded Persia during the Second World War, an officer of the British army called Lieutenant Hemming was approached by a native called Ali Mirdrekvandi. He was no different in appearance from many other poor Persians at the time. He had been brought up as a poverty-stricken peasant. His clothes were old and torn. He asked for work, but the only thing which recommended him was the fact that he could read his own language, and was trying to learn English. It seemed remarkable that a peasant could have taught himself to read. 'I have learnt about 1,000 words of English' Ali wrote to the lieutenant in his first letter. A job was found for him and, eventually, he became a 'houseboy' to a group of officers. They called him Gunga Din.

While he was working for them, Gunga Din was also busy writing. The book which he wrote was very long. But as well as that, perhaps for the amusement of the officers, many of whom are mentioned in his story, he also wrote a little book called *No Heaven for Gunga Din*. It's about a band of eighty-three officers in the year 2084. The Third World War is over. (Gunga Din calls it the 'Harvest Living War'.) At the beginning of the story the officers are marching along the Milky Way looking for the Gate of Heaven. But, in typical army style, somebody had forgotten to issue them with the Freedom Passes which will allow them to get in.

Gunga Din tells his story in his own peculiar English style, saying that they marched along 'with General Burke their commander in their front and with Gunga Din their servant in their behind.' (Gunga Din was once taught the Apostles' Creed but, instead of saying 'the communion of saints and the forgiveness of sins', he would insist on 'the communion of sins and the forgiveness of saints'.) In his story the officers have great difficulty in finding the Gate of Heaven. The normal procedure, apparently, is for souls to collect their Freedom Passes at the Judgement

Field. Some might have to serve a sentence in Hell before being allowed into Heaven. But this contingent is wandering around without observing the proper rules.

They have many amusing adventures. They come to what looks like a garden, but it turns out to be a Cloud Service Station. There they meet a Wonderful Creature who feeds them and gives them some advice. One of the officers is very upset because the Wonderful Creature has no tobacco and doesn't know what it is. In his story, Gunga Din makes fun of the officers he serves. Obviously one of them was very fond of smoking his pipe, and became irritable if he had no tobacco. The Wonderful Creature, too, has never seen men before and wants to know what kind of creatures they are. Are they goats, sheep, cats, lions, birds, snakes, leopards, lambs, bees, camels or horses? When they explain that they are men, the Wonderful Creature wants to know if they are girls, old men or old women?

The Wonderful Creature then sends the officers to the Holy Office. (Here Gunga Din is making a joke out of the fact that priests call the services they conduct 'the Holy Office'.) There they find the Holy Commanders – the Wind Commander, the Cloud Commander, the Snow Commander, the Rain Commander and the Fate Commander. The Holy Commanders ask the officers to decide which commander is the most beautiful, whose duty is the most heavy and which is the most useful to earthly creatures. They spend a morning in the Holy Office deciding. They watch the commanders as they control events on earth. A ship is sunk in the Mediterranean, a tornado devastates a Persian village, a fire sweeps through a market town, there is heavy rain throughout England for forty minutes. The officers finally vote for the Wind Commander and are surprised when the others are not annoyed. They 'kiss each other's faces'.

At the end of Gunga Din's story, all the officers are living happily in Heaven. Only Gunga Din, who has commited ten million Venial Sins and Six Mortal Sins in the course of his lifetime, is in Hell. The officers decide, one day, to visit him. When they see Gunga Din in Hell, they are very upset. 'Hell-Fire usually attacks us from supper-time until morning,' Gunga Din explains. 'By morning it has killed us and turned us to ashes. When the world becomes morning, Hell-Fire goes off and we are brought to life again.' The officers decide that this cannot go on. They stage a revolt and demand the abolition of Hell. But we are not told whether they succeed.

We don't know what happened to Gunga Din. He was last heard of in 1949. Probably, he was brought up as a Moslem, but his ideas of religion were clearly affected by the British and American officers whom he served. At the end of his book, he leaves us with his riddle: 'God loves all his creatures in one measure.' It's not clear what he meant. But he was not happy with the Christian idea that, at the end of time, some human beings will go to Hell.

QUESTIONS FOR DEBATE

1. In what ways did Gunga Din mock the British army? Do you think it was done simply for fun, or did he dislike the British officers?
2. What do you think Gunga Din meant by saying 'God loves all his creatures in one measure'?

The Modern World

Advent   (4 mins)

No festival has caught the public imagination quite like Christmas. It's easily the most convivial time of the year. A lot of people go away for Easter. The airports are jammed as they rush for a ride to the sun. But Christmas? On the whole, people stay at home. The streets are frozen like iron. Shoppers cram the pavements buying turkeys and Christmas puddings, pairs of unusable green socks and boxes of dates. We put up Christmas trees, hang streamers in our living rooms and wear paper hats at parties. There's something slightly dotty about it all. A lot of people go to church at no other time of the year. But there they all are, crowded into the parish churches at midnight as Christmas Day arrives. You would have thought that they could have found a more convenient time for their annual visit to church than at midnight in the middle of the winter.

But what are our modern Christmas celebrations about? To say the least, it's difficult to define. The New Testament has two versions of the Christmas story, one in St Matthew's gospel and the other in St Luke's. They both agree that Jesus was born in Bethlehem in the hill country of Judea, and that he was brought up in Nazareth in Galilee. But they agree on practically nothing else. Matthew says that Joseph and Mary were natives of Bethlehem in the hill country of Judea, and that Jesus was brought up in Nazareth in Galilee. Matthew says that Joseph and Mary were natives of Bethlehem, that their baby was born in a house and that he was visited by wise men from the east. Luke says that Joseph and Mary were natives of Nazareth, obliged to visit Bethlehem because the government had ordered a census. The child Jesus was born in a stable and a manger was used as his cradle. Angels on a hillside sent some shepherds to visit Jesus at his birth. In the Nativity plays performed in schools and churches at Christmas time, these two contradictory stories are somehow brought together.

To understand Christmas — indeed to understand the Nativity stories — we should look at the poetry. Poets, at their best, say things which other people find difficult to put into words. The great poem at the beginning of St John's gospel does precisely that. You may not believe in Christianity. You may have no religious beliefs at all. Yet the sheer power and magic of the words brings Christmas to life:

READER

> In the beginning was the Word, and the Word was with
> God, and the Word was God.
> The same was in the beginning with God.
> All things were made by him; and without him was not
> any thing made that was made.
> In him was life; and the life was the light of men.
> And the light shineth in darkness, and the darkness
> comprehended it not.
> There was a man sent from God whose name was John. The same came
> for a witness, to bear witness to the
> light, that all men through him might believe.
> He was not that Light, but was sent to bear witness
> to that Light.
> That was the true Light, which lighteth every man that cometh into the
> world.
> He was in the world, and the world was made by him, and the world
> knew him not.
> He came unto his own, and his own received him not. But as many
> as received him, to them gave he the power to become the sons of God,
> even to them that believe on his name:
> Which were born, not of blood, nor of the will of
> the flesh, nor of the will of man, but of God.
> And the Word was made flesh, and dwelt among us,
> (and we beheld his glory, the glory as of the only
> begotten of the Father,) full of grace and truth.

What does it mean? There are some pieces of music, the more you play them, the more you see in them. This is exactly the same. God, outside time and space, brought all things into being simply by saying his word. But the word was not simply a command. It also brought understanding, and there is no greater understanding than that. John the Baptist saw it and drew our attention to it. And the writer of St John's gospel says that he and the people with him also saw the glory of it, full of grace and truth.

QUESTIONS FOR DEBATE

1. Can you think of other examples of human dottiness at Christmas time?
2. What other ideas can you see in the poem at the beginning of St John's gospel?

Coventry Cathedral   (5 mins)

Night after night for two years during World War II, the German bombers unloaded their cargoes of destruction on the city of Coventry. Firemen struggled to put out the innumerable conflagrations which sprang up everywhere. People spent every night in the air-raid shelters, hoping that their homes would still be there the following day. Searchlights moved criss-cross through the night trying to pick out the enemy planes. Ack-ack guns spat out shells at any plane that was spotted. On Thursday 14th November, 1940, the city lost one of its greatest treasures — the magnificent fourteenth century cathedral church of St Michael. It was during the longest air-raid of any one night over any British city during the war.

A few days after the bombing, two pieces of charred wood from the roof timbers of the cathedral were tied together with wire to make a rough cross. The 'Charred Cross' is one of the treasures of the cathedral today, and stands on the stone altar at the east end of the ruins. Behind it, carved in the stone, are the simple words 'Father forgive'. The cross was, in those days of war, a sign of determination that the cathedral would be rebuilt. And from the day when the ancient building was destroyed until the day the new one was consecrated twenty-two years later, the services of the cathedral were conducted in the ruins.

The new cathedral at Coventry was consecrated on 25th May, 1962, in the presence of Her Majesty the Queen. The architect was Sir Basil Spence, and the style which he employed was something quite new in church architecture. Yet the great sweeping lines of the modern building are linked to what remain of the Mediaeval walls of the destroyed cathedral. The basic teaching of Christianity is the new life brought about by the resurrection of Jesus Christ from the dead. The ruins at Coventry are a symbol of death, yet the new cathedral is a symbol of the new life.

There is a star-shaped chapel at the new cathedral called 'The Chapel of Unity'. That, too, is a sign of new beginnings. In 1944, while there was nothing but ruins to be seen, the 'Coventry Cathedral Scheme for Christian Unity' was launched. Out of the suffering of war came the idea that there should be a chapel to which Christians of all denominations could belong. On the threshold stone is carved the words, 'THAT THEY ALL MAY BE ONE'. The long, narrow stained-glass windows were given by the German Evangelical Churches. The mosaic floor was a gift of Sweden. The Declaration that this part of the cathedral should be set apart as a Chapel of Unity was signed by the representatives of twelve different Christian nations.

By far the most astonishing feature of the new Coventry cathedral is the gigantic tapestry designed by the artist Graham Sutherland. It is the largest tapestry in the world, and was an anonymous gift paid for by a resident of the city. The design includes the symbols of the writers of the four gospels — Matthew, Mark, Luke and John. Matthew is shown as a man, Mark as a lion, Luke as a bull and John as an eagle. But the most striking feature is the figure of Christ himself. Again the theme is death and resurrection. Christ is enclosed within a coffin-like shape, yet light is shown streaming from the top of the tapestry, the hands of the figure are raised and the eyes are open — the symbols of the new life.

There is so much to see in this great modern cathedral, so much that is remarkable. In the Baptistry, a great three-ton sandstone boulder, brought from near Bethlehem, is used as a font. It arrived on Christmas Eve, 1960, with the help of the Jordanian government, the Syrian and Lebanese transport system, the Prince Line Steamship Company and many others. It was a gift of many lands, a stone used to celebrate the baptism of any child, from near the birthplace of the child born at Christmas.

At the south entrance of the cathedral hangs Jacob Epstein's sculpture of St Michael in his struggle with the devil. The new cathedral, like the fourteenth century building which it replaced, is dedicated to St Michael. The sculpture is a sign of the age-old struggle between good and evil — the theme of this building time and time again.

QUESTIONS FOR DEBATE

1. Why is the Charred Cross one of the treasures of modern Coventry Cathedral?
2. Why was it particularly important that the German Evangelical Churches should give something to Coventry Cathedral?

The problem of war   (5 mins)

READER
> 'When the blast of war blows in our ears,
> Then imitate the action of a tiger;
> Stiffen the sinews, conjure up the blood,
> Disguise fair nature with hard-favoured rage . . .
> Now set the teeth and stretch the nostril wide,
> Hold hard the breath, and bend up every spirit
> To its full height! On, on you noblest English!
> . . . Be copy now of men of grosser blood,
> And teach them how to war.'

That is an edited version of a famous speech from Shakespeare's 'King Henry V'. Such literature has a noble ancestry. When Homer wrote of the siege of Troy — of Agamemnon, of Achilles and Hector — he described the epic heroes of ancient Greece in much the same sort of language, glorifying war itself. Any Hollywood film director, about to make a 'cowboy and Indian' film, should go back to read the Iliad. The setting may have been different, but the quality of the heroes remains much the same. Or 'cowboy and Indian' films could be based just as easily on the legends of King Arthur and the knights of the Round Table. It is a part of human nature to admire and to wonder at the deeds of mighty men. And the function of poetry itself has been described as the celebration of heroes. Certainly, the earliest poetry in any literature concerns great battles and mighty conquests.

  But there is another side of the coin:

READER
> With proud thanksgiving, a mother for her children,
>   England mourns for her dead across the sea.
> Flesh of her flesh they were, spirit of her spirit,
>   Fallen in the cause of the free.
>
> Solemn the drums thrill: Death august and royal
>   Sings sorrow up into immortal spheres.
> There is a music in the midst of desolation
>   And a glory that shines upon our tears.

That is an extract from Laurence Binyon's famous poem 'For the fallen' — mourning the men who died in the First World War. The best known part of it is recited each year at war memorials on Armistice Sunday:

READER

They shall grow not old, as we that are left grow old;
Age shall not weary them, nor the years condemn,
At the going down of the sun and in the morning
We will remember them.

Binyon saw the men who died in terms of a heroic tragedy. Again, that is an emotion which has a long and venerable history. The churches of this country contain many memorials full of praise for the heroic dead, killed in war.

Yet, particularly with the First World War, another reaction to war itself began to set in:

READER

Red lips are not so red
As the stained stones kissed by the English dead.
Kindness of wooed and wooer
Seems shame to their love pure.
O Love, your eyes lose their lure
When I behold eyes blinded in my stead!

Here, the young Wilfred Owen is writing to the girl of his dreams − but this is no romantic poem. Much as he wants her and loves her, the sheer horror of the dead men around him in the trenches puts him off:

READER

...your eyes lose their lure
When I behold eyes blinded in my stead!

Those dead men could quite easily have been him. Indeed Owen himself was later to die in the trenches. On a personal level, war is horrific − destructive not just of human bodies but of the simple, normal things that a young man wants − such as a girl friend. It was out of such writings that a new spirit arose in this century. People began to talk of the avoidance of war − and with it came the League of

Nations. 'Better', said Winston Churchill at the end of the Second World War, 'jaw, jaw than war, war'.

Of course the League of Nations and, later, the United Nations could not always work. Sometimes the ways of thinking of people thrown up against each other are so at variance, so conflicting, that life itself is carried on with extreme difficulty. It is true of Cyprus, divided between Greek and Turk, or the Holy Land, divided between Jew and Palestinian, or Northern Ireland, divided between Catholic and Protestant. In theory, peoples of different cultures should be able to live in toleration and in peace. In practice, there are always extremists willing to throw the petrol bomb or barricade the streets.

QUESTIONS FOR DEBATE

1. It is now many years since the end of the Second World War. Should churches continue to hold memorial services on Armistice Sunday?
2. Can you think of ways of helping people to be more tolerant?

A Christmas nightmare   (6 mins)

In his dream, the man was walking through wild country in deep snow. It wasn't at all clear where he was going, but a feeling of near panic drove him on. He clambered over dry-stone walls, careful not to dislodge the topmost stones. Many an ankle has been bruised or broken by a stone falling from a wall. Below was a wide valley and, in the distance, the serrated peaks of a range of mountains. Something told him that they were his destination. But there was not a house in sight − no welcoming lights nor any sign of civilization. He would have rejoiced to see the work-a-day swish of traffic on a main road, telegraph posts and roadmen digging the highway for Christmas. Christmas? Ah yes, he remembered now. It was Christmas − trees and candles and carols, old Wenceslas on his annual outing to rescue 'yonder peasant'.

He saw the peasant in the distance, an old man gnarled as an oak tree and hump-backed, chopping firewood in a derelict farmyard. The ancient farmhouse, tucked into the landscape, had escaped his attention up to that point. As he worked his way down the hillside, the wind blew with even greater vehemence and a wild thin snow wrapped itself around his face so that he could not look ahead. He watched his heavy wellingtons clump into the creamy layer of snow beneath his feet. Then he noticed something else. A second pair of footsteps appeared alongside his own. He stopped to examine this phenomenon. The other footsteps stopped as well. He experimented. His right foot went forward and sank into the snow. Immediately, about a yard to the right, a footprint identical in shape and size to his own appeared. He took a few paces forward, then looked back. They were already filling with snow, but he could see distinctly the traces of two pairs of footsteps going away into the distance.

These extra footsteps worried him at first. He had never believed in ghosts, nor did he wish to believe in them. Then a feeling of resentment took over. Was he really going to spend the rest of his life making two pairs of footsteps everywhere he went? People would avoid him, and television producers would take films of him. He had no desire whatsoever to become a freak for public entertainment. He stopped and stood for a moment, thinking about it in the white world where driving snowflakes made his cheeks smart and the wind banged in his ears. He would ask the peasant, he decided. Perhaps an old man would know what to do. So he continued down to the track which led into the farmyard, ignoring the footsteps which worked their way along beside him. Sometimes he thought he could actually hear them as they did so. But that might have been his imagination.

'Terrible day,' he said to the old man. The old fellow was working beneath a shelter of corrugated iron. He brought his axe down on a log. It split, and he bent down to pick up the two halves. Then he turned. 'The day's all right,' he said. 'It's God's day. But the weather's not very good. Are you coming inside?' The man followed him across the farmyard and into the bare quarry-tiled kitchen. A large iron range sent flames up the open gash of the chimney. Horse brasses twinkled on the walls and shadows lurked in the corners. Apart from the fire, there seemed to be no source of light. The man went over to warm himself. The old fellow produced a steaming tin mug filled with tea. 'You have sugar?'

There was something unreal about it. Where was he? What was he doing? He had spent his childhood in the country, and had often visited farmhouses like this. But he knew that farm kitchens of such a style had long disappeared, the iron ranges replaced with modern cookers, the shadows in the corners dissipated in the steady glare of electric light. The pleasant, antique atmosphere pleased him, and he sat and talked to the old man for some time. They spoke mostly of sheep lost in snowdrifts on the barren hillsides, and the hunting foxes which plagued the farms. Somehow, it took him a long time to come round to the question of the footsteps. When he did mention them, the old man showed no surprise. 'It's God,' he said. 'He walks beside you — that's all.'

Then, suddenly, the man knew he must go. There was no explanation for it — only an insistent urgency which told him. He rose, shook hands with the old man, pulled his coat around himself and departed. It was still snowing. Evening was drawing in. He watched the footsteps and was glad of them now. After all, there was no need for fear, was there? Not if God was with him. When he came to the base of the hills, the going suddenly became much rougher. He scrambled up untidy, rambling scree, in places as slippery as a glacier. Sometimes he dislodged a boulder which bounced out of sight below him in an instant. He stopped, panting, his heart thumping with the exertion. Then he noticed something. The other footsteps had disappeared. Panic! He froze. He forced a leg forward. It slipped. He fell on his knees, furiously grasping the rocks with his hands to avoid a fall.

It took hours, that climb. At last the man, cold, wet and shivery arrived over the brow. The going was easier now, and not far away were the lights of a little inn. He suddenly felt better, imagining the warm fire and the good country food. As he swung across the fields in that direction, he noticed. The footsteps were back!

In his dream, the man was in heaven. He did not know how. He could not see God; he knew that God was there. 'They were your footsteps, weren't they?' he said. 'Yes,' said God. Suddenly, the man was angry. 'But why did you desert me when the going got tough?' 'I didn't,' said God, 'I carried you.'

QUESTIONS FOR DEBATE

1. Do you think dreams sometimes have meanings?
2. In what ways are the stories of Christmas mixed into the man's dream?

The lost continent of Atlantis   (4 mins)

Over two thousand years ago, the great Greek philosopher Plato described a vanished continent called Atlantis. He went into great detail about life in Atlantis — information which he said had been taken from ancient Egyptian writings. He described the intricate man-made canal system, the ports and the mighty fleet of ships, the temples and the profusion of gold, the methods of agriculture and husbandry of animals, the government, the methods of trade. Plato's Atlantis was a truly mighty country, ruling over surrounding civilizations with absolute power. Then, according to Plato, it sank with all its people into the sea:

READER

> Here occured violent earthquakes and floods, and in a single day and night of rain all your warlike men in a body sank into the earth, and the island of Atlantis in like manner disappeared, and was sunk beneath the seas.

But could such an advanced civilization have existed thousands of years before the rise of ancient Egypt? At the time when Atlantis was said to be flourishing, human beings generally lived in caves and survived by hunting. Yet Plato asks us to accept the idea that there existed a highly advanced culture somewhere in the middle of the Atlantic Ocean. It sounds like a flight of imagination. Yet, surprisingly, there are some tantalizing facts in support of Plato's story.

Legends which speak of a very ancient continent and a people destroyed by some great disaster exist among many peoples living in lands bordering the Atlantic Ocean. The tribes of north-west Africa, for instance, speak of the Atlantes. The tribes of another part of Africa remember Attala. Centuries ago, the South American Aztecs spoke of Aztlan, and the Basques of France and Spain have legends about Atlaintika. The Gauls of France and the Celts of Britain spoke of Avalon. All these legends date from before recorded history. The name of the Atlantic Ocean itself seems to be a memory of the lost continent.

There are many theories about Atlantis. Another legend is that of the Great Flood described in the Bible. Noah collected into the ark two of each of all the animals of the world, and thus he saved them. This story is not exclusive to the Bible. It exists in one form or another in every major religion throughout the world. It is tempting to think that this might be the collective memory of the great flood of water that destroyed Atlantis.

Such theories are, of course, speculation. But there are interesting facts concerning islands in the Atlantic which might be considered as evidence of the existence of Atlantis. Islands such as the Canaries, the Bahamas and the Azores could well have been the mountain tops of the sunken continent. Certain facts about these islands seem to support such speculations. The inhabitants of the Canaries, for instance, when the islands were discovered by the Spanish in 1395, were surprised to find that other people still lived on the earth. They regarded themselves as the only survivors of a great flood which had destroyed the whole world. These islands were, they said, the tops of the mountains. Surprisingly for island dwellers, their fear of water was such that they had no boats at all. Tall, white-skinned and blond-haired, they were wiped out by the Spanish.

Surprising links have been found between peoples of the west and east sides of the Atlantic. Were there links between them thousands of years before Columbus' famous crossing? Certain American Indian words bear a striking resemblance to words from cultures with no apparent connexion. The American Indian word for king is 'malku'; the Hebrew word is 'melekh'. The American Indian word for home is 'oko'; the Greek word is 'oika'. There are many such trans-Atlantic correspondences. The Aztecs, for instance, were found to play the Persian game of parcheesi, calling it 'patolli'.

The date suggested for the end of Atlantis coincides with the end of the Ice Age, some eleven thousand years ago. It is indeed possible that the land was drowned by the melting glaciers. Discoveries have been made below sea level near the islands of the Azores, the Bahamas and the Canaries to show that the sea level was once very much lower than it is today. This is the area called the mid-Atlantic ridge which, under the water, rises nine thousand feet above the sea floor. If the sea level were lowered sufficiently to uncover this ridge, a large continent would indeed be formed. Perhaps it is also significant that this is an area of instability in the earth's crust where volcanic activity is common.

In recent years pilots flying over this area have often claimed to have seen regular shapes beneath the waters suggesting submerged buildings and walls. Submarines have even photographed what appear to be man-made structures at a very great depth. A long heavily-encrusted structure stretches out for a considerable distance under the sea at Bimini in the Bahamas. The straightness of the structure suggests a wall or a road. Could such a phenomenon have occurred naturally? Certainly, man-made artifacts have been discovered on the sea bed around these islands. The best scientific evidence has come from soil samples taken from the mid-Atlantic ridge. In these have been found the remains of volcanic ash, and of animal and plant life from ten to twelve thousand years ago.

Many of these discoveries have been made very recently, often completely by accident. But no detailed survey has, as yet, been made. Whether these underwater discoveries point to the lost Atlantis or merely to islands that were once somewhat larger than they are now will not be known until a more comprehensive study has been undertaken. But it is clear that a mystery lurks under the waters of the Atlantic waiting for the time when we will find out.

QUESTIONS FOR DEBATE

1. Do you think that Atlantis really did exist?
2. Suggest reasons why writers might enjoy making up a lost continent.

The duck-decoy   (5 mins)

At Boarstall in Buckinghamshire there is a curious lake. It lies in a woodland park, and at first the visitor might not notice anything unusual. The park is a favourite haunt of bird watchers, and you see them, binoculars in hand, wandering the pathways. What is unusual, however, is that a small water channel runs away in a curve from the lake. It is quite wide where it meets the lake, but the channel gradually becomes narrower and narrower as it runs into the woodland. And over the channel there are iron hoops which support a net. The visitor will guess that this channel amounts to a kind of trap, but it is difficult to imagine how it works.

Alongside the channel there is a series of pieces of close-boarded fence, running on the curved line of the cut. Each piece of fencing stands independent of the others, and there are gaps between them. These are the clues to the trap. Particularly in the winter months, there are wild ducks of a great many varieties on the lake — mallards, mandarins, polchards. When these ducks are to be lured into the net-covered water channels, a man appears with a dog specially bred to look like a fox. It is a remarkably funny sight. The ducks look at the dog and, believing it to be a fox, set up a great commotion. They feel secure as they float on the surface of the water, able to hurl abuse at their natural enemy, the fox. There are great quackings and splashings. And they all move in the direction of the dog to emphasize the point. I imagine, if we understood duck language, we would hear a great many duck 'four letter words'.

The dog has been trained to take advantage of the fascination which his appearance has for the ducks. He begins to move in and out between the pieces of close-boarded fence running alongside the water channel. Now the ducks see him, now they don't. Duck curiosity is aroused. 'Where's he gone? Ah, there he is!' As the dog worms his way in and out of the fences, he lures the ducks further and further up the water channel until they are trapped in the net. The duck-decoy works because it takes advantage of duck psychology.

The earliest example of one of these duck-decoys was in St James' Park in London in the seventeenth century. The purpose was to supply the royal household with a plentiful supply of fresh duck. Nowadays, the duck-decoy at Boarstall is owned by the Wildfowl Trust and is used to trap ducks so that a small plastic ring can be put on one of their legs. Ducks migrate to many different countries and travel astonishing distances. The idea of ringing them is to trace their movements. Ducks from Boarstall have been found as far away as Russia. They have also been found served in London restaurants.

The duck-decoy is an amazing example of human ingenuity from a bygone age. I wonder who first noticed that ducks become so abusive at the sight of a fox that they forget to notice where they are going? And I wonder who thought out this way of taking advantage of their indignation? The duck-decoy was meant to serve the dinner table in times past. Yet it is an arrangement very useful to the Wildfowl Trust. The wardens are able to capture the ducks without hurting them in any way.

QUESTIONS FOR DEBATE

1. Can you think of other examples of ingenious devices from a bygone age? Are they different from the kinds of things we invent nowadays?
2. Is it wrong to deceive the ducks in this manner — or is it much more serious to deceive people?

Gandhi   (5 mins)

In 1914, the South African statesman General Smuts wrote to a friend: 'The saint has left our shores, I hope for ever'. He was referring to Mohandas Gandhi who had caused the South African authorities such trouble. Yet nobody could have predicted that the reserved, quiet young man of a few years earlier would shake the foundations of a government of the British Empire. Gandhi was born in 1869, the son of the chief minister of Gujerat in western India. His mother was entirely absorbed in a strict type of Hindu religion which regarded everything in the universe as eternal, and in which non-violence to living creatures was a basic principle. Gandhi was therefore brought up as a vegetarian. There was to be no violence to animals just so that he could eat. Yet there was nothing particularly remarkable about him when he was young. He was never brilliant at school, nor had he any great interest in sport. His real pleasure was to go for long, solitary walks. He was married at the age of thirteen.

Gandhi would have liked to have become a doctor, but his family felt that he should follow in his father's footsteps. It meant training as a barrister, and led to his visit to England at the age of nineteen. He joined the Inner Temple, one of the four London law colleges. He found it a painful struggle to adapt himself to western food and dress, and his vegetarianism was at first a source of embarrassment to him. Eventually, he joined the London Vegetarian Society and met not only people with strange ideas about food, but also famous rebels like George Bernard Shaw. Among these people, there was a great deal of idealism, and many of them were very critical of the political ideas of the time.

When Gandhi returned to India in 1891, he found that it was difficult to obtain a job. There were a great many young Indian barristers, and he was too shy a man to elbow his way in. He was turned down too when he applied for a job as a part-time teacher. In the end, he gratefully accepted a year's contract with an Indian firm in Natal, South Africa. Gandhi was astonished at the treatment he received in South Africa. Very soon after his arrival, he was thrown violently off a train while travelling to Pretoria – because he was sitting in a part of the train reserved for the whites. Later on the same journey, he was beaten up by the driver of a stage coach because he would not give up his seat to a white passenger.

This was common treatment for Indians in South Africa at the time. The Indians had first migrated to South Africa in the 1860s, to work in the sugar plantations. In Gandhi's time, there were many Indians working as traders or as labourers. They were used to such treatment, but Gandhi was not. His reaction was surprising. This shy, ungainly man suddenly became determined to defend his dignity as an Indian and as a member of the human race. No human being should be treated as inferior to any other. He tried to encourage his fellow Indians to assert their rights.

But Gandhi had no intention of staying in South Africa to carry out the fight himself. Things changed at a party which was held in his honour when he was about to return to India. He happened to glance at a copy of the 'Natal Mercury'. There was a report in that newspaper that the government of Natal was considering depriving Indians of the right to vote. He was horrified, and decided that he must stay. Up to this point, Gandhi had found speech-making a terrifying experience, and had showed very little interest in politics. Overnight he became a skilled political campaigner. He drafted petitions to the Natal authorities and to the British government. In 1894, he founded the Natal Indian Congress to represent his compatriots and became its very hardworking secretary. Soon important newspapers, such as 'The Times' in London and 'The Statesman and Englishman' in Calcutta were commenting on the grievances of the Natal Indians.

In 1896, Gandhi went to India to collect his wife and children. He also met important Indian political leaders, and encouraged them to support his cause. The accounts in the South African newspapers of his visit to India caused anger in some white quarters. When he arrived back in Durban in January, 1897, he was assaulted by a white crowd. The British cabinet was so alarmed at what had happened that messages were sent to Natal asking that the guilty men should be prosecuted. But Gandhi refused to take any revenge. He would not use a court of law for his own satisfaction.

During the Boer War, Gandhi organized his followers to support the British colonial authorities in Natal. He believed that, if the Indians expected to be treated as full citizens, they were also bound to defend the colony. It is a tribute to the remarkable power of the man that he led Indians to support a government they regarded as an oppressor. The British victory in the Boer War, though, did little to improve the lot of the Indians. In 1906, the Transvaal government decided that all Indians must be registered. Under Gandhi's leadership, at a mass protest meeting at Johannesburg, the Indians took a pledge to defy the new law and to accept any punishments meted out as a result. This approach was at the heart of Gandhi's ideas. Wrongs could be righted, not by inflicting punishment but by being prepared to suffer for them. By 1913, hundreds of Indian men and women were in prison for defying the registration laws. Indian workers in the mines were on strike. They faced flogging and imprisonment. But if the pressure on the Indian community was great, the pressure on the South African government was even greater. International opinion, particularly in Britain and in India, forced General Smuts to negotiate with Gandhi. A compromise was worked out.

Although Gandhi was born in the nineteenth century, he became a major influence on the modern world, and the effect of his work is still felt today. India, like South Africa, was a British colony for most of Gandhi's lifetime. But on his return, he began to work towards home rule for the sub-continent. Gandhi's method of passive resistance was not a means of gaining quick results, and often involved a great deal of personal suffering. Home rule did not come to India until 1947, at the end of World War II. But the long, unceasing years of struggle in the life of Gandhi were behind it. In January 1948, on his way to an evening prayer meeting, Gandhi was shot down by a young Hindu fanatic.

QUESTIONS FOR DEBATE

1. Would you call Gandhi a religious man?
2. Why does passive resistance take a long time to have any effect in politics?

The bones of St Peter   (7 mins)

According to the New Testament, Simon Peter was the disciple to whom Jesus gave the keys of the Kingdom of Heaven. After Jesus' time, he became the leader of the early Church. In the last chapter of St John's gospel, Jesus seems to predict that Peter will die by crucifixion. But there is no account of his death in the New Testament. Peter just fades from the scene and is mentioned no more. We are told in later documents that Mark was Peter's attendant when he conducted Christian services in first century Rome. But the stories of Peter's death and burial are uncorroborated legend. Yet a series of discoveries made in the nineteen thirties and forties do seem to supply the information about Peter's death which the New Testament omits.

It seems reasonable to believe that Peter died in Rome in the A.D. sixties. There are many traditions concerning his death. They say that he was condemned to death by crucifixion, but that he asked to be crucified upside down, feeling himself unworthy to die in the same way as Jesus himself. The traditions say that he was executed on Vatican Hill and that his body was stolen away by the Christians and buried secretly in the middle of a pagan graveyard. The truth about his resting place, so it is claimed, was known only to a very few select people.

It is certainly true that, for many years after Peter's time, it was dangerous to be a Christian in Rome. Many successive Roman administrations persecuted members of the Church. It explains why Peter's burial place was likely to remain one of the secrets of the Christian community. It was only when the emperor Constantine came to power and was converted to Christianity that a permanent change took place. With a Christian emperor on the throne, Christianity became the official religion of the empire. In 330 A.D., Constantine was shown what was believed to be the site of Peter's grave. There he erected the great Basilica of St Peter, the high altar situated directly over the grave. This is the most generally accepted tradition about the final resting place of St Peter.

Underneath the Basilica of St Peter, there is a long, low room called the Sacred Grotto. In 1939, it was decided to lower the floor of this room in order to convert it into a chapel. Digging down, the builders came across the top of a rectangle of brick walls, twenty-two feet long by twenty feet wide. Surprised by this discovery, they dug further and found that it was a roofless building, plastered and ornately painted on the inside. Further excavation proved that it was an excellently-preserved Roman tomb of about 150 A.D. It contained cremation urns and a Christian grave. Outside this building, more graves were uncovered. It became clear that the builders had stumbled across a major archaeological find.

With the permission of the Pope, work on lowering the floor was abandoned and archaeological excavation took over. The Pope instructed that they should not disturb the ground underneath the high altar itself. It became clear that the whole area had been a very large graveyard. There were many more tombs, and they found the remains of little roads and alleyways between the graves. On the walls of one pagan tomb they were excited to discover crude cartoon drawings of Christ and St Peter. There was some indecipherable writing beneath.

After some ten months of work, the archaeologists had uncovered nineteen tombs. The Pope then gave them permission to investigate beneath the high altar itself. Some historical information was already available about this area. It was known that the present altar was a sixteenth century addition, and that beneath it was a sixth century altar. It was also thought that Constantine's original altar was below that. The excavators knew that the Saracens had despoiled the grave in 846 A.D., but what damage they had done nobody knew.

It was planned to approach the area through an underground chapel behind the altar. The wall protecting the grave was removed. They then came across a white marble wall and, behind it, a red plaster wall. Here they found the sixth century altar. They then tried to enter from another angle. Again they came across the marble wall. This clearly surrounded the whole area. Once again there was the red plaster wall behind it. But this time there was also a blue wall on which was scratched strange markings and the names of people. It became clear that both the red and the blue walls were more ancient than Constantine's basilica.

Upon further inspection the archaeologists could see that the red wall had once made up one side of a rectangular courtyard. At the centre of this wall were the remains of a stone canopy. It had been damaged, very likely by the Saracens. The blue wall stood to one side of this canopy at right angles to the red wall. It had apparently been erected later to strengthen the red wall where a crack had appeared. Constantine had enclosed this little shrine with his white marble wall. The red and the blue walls were dated from the mid-second century − within a hundred years of Peter's death.

Beneath the canopied monument the archaeologists discovered human bones. They turned out to be the remains of a number of individuals. Then, inside a small hollow in the blue wall they came across a secret hiding place. Here were the bones of an old man, probably in his late sixties, heavily built and around five feet seven tall. Scratched on the plaster within this niche were the words 'PETROS ENI' − 'Peter is within'. A study of the soil samples from within the niche showed that this body had once lain in the ground below the red wall, and had later been removed to the niche.

An expert was brought in to study the writings. The inscription below the cartoons of Christ and St Peter was badly faded and the plaster was chipped. Careful reconstruction showed that it read, 'Peter pray Christ Jesus for the holy Christian men buried near your body'. Here was a definite reference to Peter's burial. The scratches on the blue wall posed a different problem. They could be read easily enough, but no one knew what they meant. Finally their significance became clear. Here was a sort of coded prayer. The writings on this wall supported the traditions about the death and burial of St Peter. If he had been executed as a criminal, his body would normally have been burnt. But, as the traditions tell, it was stolen away and buried in secret. In the midst of these pagan tombs the location of the grave was known to very few. But those who did know wanted to leave their prayers there — hence the scratchings in code on the wall. To any passer-by they would have seemed a meaningless groups of letters, but to the small Christian community they had a definite and deep significance. But why had Peter's body been removed from the ground and hidden in the blue wall? It was probably hidden there during a time of particular danger. This is where the bones of St Peter — if that is what they are — still lie today.

QUESTIONS FOR DEBATE

1. Can you suggest reasons why Peter's grave was important to the early Christians?
2. Does the archaeology prove that the bones of St Peter have been discovered?

The immigrants   (4 mins)

The history of Britain has always involved the coming of immigrants. Our knowledge of history before the arrival of the Romans has been gained to a large extent from the work of the archaeologists. The lack of written records means that there are many gaps in our information. Yet there is clear archaeological evidence of the arrival in ancient Britain of many different peoples at different times. Until late in the Middle Stone Age in the sixth millenium B.C., Britain was part of the European landmass. Wandering tribes of hunters moved freely in from the continent. Then, with the cutting of the landbridge, Britain became an island and from then on, for the most part, developed independently of the rest of Europe.

In about 4,000 B.C., Neolithic invaders from the coasts of western Europe were the first to introduce farming into Britain. About two thousand years later, there came another large body of immigrants. Their skulls are different in appearance from the Neolithic people, and they have been called Beaker people because they often buried drinking vessels in the graves. They were the first people to develop the mining of gold and copper. Trade expanded enormously. Stonehenge was first built by the Neolithic people, but it was greatly enlarged and improved by the Beaker people. The two cultures obviously shared the same kind of religious beliefs.

Probably in the seventh century B.C., Celtic tribes from central Europe began to arrive in Britain. They built some of the earliest hill forts, and distinctive Celtic-style farms began to appear. They constructed small fields, circular houses and storage pits for grain. Some of the finest examples of prehistoric art to survive in Britain were produced by the Celts. They made elaborately decorated swords, scabbards, shields and helmets, typical of continental Celtic art yet with a peculiarly British style.

Although these many different peoples arriving on the shores of Britain had their own characteristics, there was a continuous merging of populations. There may have been many battles at various times between newcomers and natives, but there was also intermarriage. Julius Caesar invaded Britain in 55 B.C. and came again in the following year. He was the first to write a coherent account of the country. Other later Roman historians tell us a great deal about Roman Britain and its inhabitants. The country was divided geographically, each region being under the control of a particular tribe. The people in those tribes were clearly of mixed ancestry, descendants of the various waves of invaders.

The Roman historians tell us that there was a marked contrast between the Britons who lived in the rich farming lowlands and those who lived in the hills. The lowlanders were perfectly happy to accept and appreciate the Roman way of life. But the dwellers in the hill country — places like Scotland and Wales — resisted Roman power and saw it as a threat to freedom. Evidence of the influence of the Romans, their buildings and their culture, is to be found in many places in Britain. The remains of Roman villas are tourist attractions, and many of the routes followed by modern roads were originally chosen by the Roman engineers.

The withdrawal of the legions as Rome itself came under threat was followed in the fifth and sixth centuries by the coming of new continental invaders — the Saxons, the Angles, the Danes and many other peoples of Northern European origin. The outcome was clearly very similar to that of the earlier developments. There were battles with the newcomers, but there was also intermarriage and the merging of populations. Only in the extremities of Britain — places like Wales, Scotland and Cornwall — did the earlier cultures survive and continue to develop. After the coming of the Anglo-Saxons, Britain was conquered only one more time — by William, Duke of Normandy in 1066. At first there was a sharp distinction between the natives and their Norman rulers. But as with earlier newcomers, gradually they merged with the rest of the population.

Britain may not have been conquered by foreigners since 1066, but immigration has continued nevertheless. There have been many reasons for it. Britain has been used as a haven for people escaping from trouble elsewhere. The persecution of the Hugenots in France in the later part of the seventeenth century, for instance, brought many of them to Britain. And, as recently as 1965, Hungarian refugees arrived, fleeing from the reimposition of Soviet power in their own country.

But in this century, particularly in the era after World War II, immigration into Britain has been largely for financial reasons. Peoples from many of Britain's former colonies — India, Pakistan, the Carribean islands in particular — have come to settle and to take jobs. As with earlier immigrants, they have brought with them a further diversity of cultures. Mosques, and Sikh and Hindu temples can be found in many of our towns and cities. And some of our popular music has been influenced by Indian or West Indian styles. In recent years, successive British governments have been concerned to restrict such immigration, fearing that the clash of cultures will lead to violence. Certainly, particularly in some of the inner cities, there has been trouble between different communities. Yet, if the past is any guide to the future, the pattern that is likely to emerge will involve yet again the merging of populations.

QUESTIONS FOR DEBATE

1. In what ways does immigration into Britain benefit the country?
2. Is there evidence that the immigrants into Britain since World War II are merging into the general population?